MEN'S
STYLE

RUSSELL SMITH **MEN'S**

STYLE

THE THINKING MAN'S GUIDE TO DRESS

Illustrations by
Edwin Fotheringham

Library and Archives Canada Cataloguing in Publication

Smith, Russell, 1963-
    Men's style : the thinking man's guide to dress / Russell Smith.

Includes index.
ISBN 0-7710-8125-1

    1. Men's clothing.   2. Fashion.   I. Title.   II. Title: Style.

TT617.S62 2005   646'.32   C2005-902307-4

We acknowledge the financial support of the Government of Canada through the Book Publishing Industry Development Program and that of the Government of Ontario through the Ontario Media Development Corporation's Ontario Book Initiative. We further acknowledge the support of the Canada Council for the Arts and the Ontario Arts Council for our publishing program.

Typeset in Sabon by M&S, Toronto
Printed and bound in Canada

This book is printed on acid-free paper that is 100% recycled, ancient-forest friendly (40% post-consumer recycled).

McClelland & Stewart Ltd.
The Canadian Publishers
481 University Avenue
Toronto, Ontario
M5G 2E9
www.mcclelland.com

1 2 3 4 5   09 08 07 06 05

For Mitty Smith

CONTENTS

WHY BOTHER?

"There are moments, Jeeves,
when one asks oneself, 'Do trousers matter?'"
"The mood will pass, sir."

– P.G. WODEHOUSE

This is the most fundamental question of all, and it had best be settled off the top. Who cares? If I confess – even to myself – an interest in the superficial, am I not admitting to superficiality generally? Am I not admitting my failure to qualify as a practical man, as the kind of quiet and sober man who has built empires and scored winning touchdowns, the wholesome but unassuming man that this continent most values?

For let's admit it, it is in North America that this thought worries us most. This is still a fundamentally Protestant and democratic place, a place which defines a man, quite sensibly, by what he accomplishes, not by how he appears. The land's hostility, the brutal task of producing and building while surviving in such vastness, makes even art and culture low priorities: at best a luxury; at worst morally suspect, the indulgent pursuit of idlers. This distrust we see demonstrated whenever our publicly funded galleries make a purchase.

If art-making is suspect here, then think what a rocky foothold have the more frivolous pursuits of ornamentation, the trivially aesthetic. What could be more condescending in, say, academic life than to call someone, man or woman, fashionable? Trendy, perhaps, would be worse, since it clearly means unsubstantial; slacker, which means the same thing, is definitely worse; vain maybe, since it connotes self-centredness – but all are indeed associated with the dreaded fashion. Dandy is the worst of all, signifying a lack of all that gets the harvest done, the skyscraper built: manliness, team spirit, co-operation, self-effacement, simple practicality. How does a dandy build a railroad?

Curiously, this queasiness about appearing to take an interest in the aesthetic comes from both the right and the left. And it comes from both men and women.

The old-fashioned opposition originates in simple social conservatism: sensuality is unseemly in a man – its ultimate manifestation, flamboyance, an embarrassment. And then of course there's homosexuality, which is, as heroin addiction is to marijuana smoking, the logical end of such an unhealthy preoccupation. Even more offensive than homosexuality is mere effeminacy, retreat of the weak-willed, of the boys afraid to join the rugby game or buffalo hunt.

Conservative women are just as likely to be embarrassed by overly beautiful or tasteful men. Taste itself seems like a feminine trait to many women. I have heard women of all ages – particularly young women from wealthy suburbs who are attending exclusive universities – sneering at guys who "dress up," meaning those who wear anything but jeans and a T-shirt. "Trying too hard," say the girls with manicured nails and sun-lamp tans. For more formal occasions, they would put their men in khaki trousers and polo shirts. Bland is attractive to conservative women – it seems reliable. Maybe it reminds them of their dads.

The socialist opposition has a slightly more complicated origin but ends in the same place. The sensitive scorner of fashion is concerned about elitism, about consumerism, about materialism generally. He thinks it ridiculous that people should spend so much money on frippery, when people are all basically the same and so many in the world are starving. He thinks that distinctions in clothing lead to distinctions in social class, which is an injustice to be eliminated, if possible, or at least masked. He is the type who defiantly wears his old sweater to a black-tie gala as some kind of inarticulately political protest.

The socialist/sensitive opposition also often takes the shape of one argument: a distaste for the false.

"BLAND is attractive to CONSERVATIVE women – it seems RELIABLE. Maybe it REMINDS them of their DADS."

What is good is natural and pure; what is bad is artificial and pretend. The word *pretentious* comes up frequently in reference to metropolitan social life: it refers to fancy restaurants and martini bars, and especially to any nightclub with a barrier of velvet ropes before its door, and a doorman with a clipboard. People who dress up are "pretentious" – meaning, I think, that they are pretending to be better than the rest of us.

Actually I'm not sure what "pretentious" really means in this context; it has become an all-purpose insult among those opposed to sophistication, exactly what "gay" means on the playground. In my experience, at least in Canada, where I grew up, "pretentious" tends to mean someone who gets better marks than you do. (Which is what "gay" means on playgrounds, too.)

I have struggled through many a tofu-heavy dinner party to convince the detractors (*real* people they, unaffected people) of what really goes on behind those velvet ropes – that there is in fact little pretense, that no one inside is pretending to be anyone else. In a dark and fashionable bar, there are rarely conversations about books that people have pretended to read or ideas people have pretended to understand; indeed, there are rarely conversations at all. No one would claim otherwise. The dark and fashionable bar is a place for the intercourse of surfaces.

But there we have it: surfaces, the superficial –

that, we all know, is inherently ungood. That is shallow. Isn't it?

Let us consider music, something usually not thought to be shallow. I know little about the finer points of music – can't read it, never studied it, never played an instrument – and yet I love the works of certain composers. The pleasure I get from them is intense and physical – and intellectual, too, since I know enough to compare their structural and textural qualities. I know that Brahms, say, is from an earlier historical period than Shostakovich, and since I studied history in high school I know that Brahms's formal preoccupations and the general tone of his music match those of his era, and ditto for Shostakovich.

So it's pleasant to listen to Shostakovich's music and be thrilled by it and also think about it as modernist music as opposed to Romantic. All this is tied up together; I can't separate the intellectual and the visceral. And yet there's no question that I like the surface, I like the pretty effects of Shostakovich and Brahms. It's not a verbal thing. And I can't tell you exactly what Brahms is doing that is different from what Shostakovich is doing, I can only describe it in vague emotional metaphors, the way I would describe the flavours of Bordeaux and Rioja.

The same goes for Matisse and Uccello and Vermeer. I've never painted, so I don't understand the importance of this colour and that technique. The colours are pretty. I like the surface, the rich materiality of it. I crave Matisse as I crave a silk tie or a plummy Burgundy.

But I can say that and not be shallow. Matisse, say the encyclopedias, is not shallow. Discussing Matisse as a sensual stimulus on a sensitive palate – my psyche – is also not shallow. When I talk about fashion and go to nightclubs, I am shallow.

This does not make sense.

Both left and right oppositions stem fundamentally, I think, from a religious impulse – specifically from religious injunctions to modesty. I wish the left wing were as honest about this as the right wing is. If you feel that those injunctions are outdated and not useful, then you may enjoy the following advice without guilt.

And even if you agree with the religious premise, fear not: I would argue that it is possible to be attractive and modest at the same time; indeed, I will be consistently on the lookout, in these pages, for the overly flamboyant and the tacky – for too much of the tie-bar and the signet ring – in an effort to eradicate them from all of our lives. And of course it is possible to be attractive and religious at the same time. (People who have spent time in Catholic countries know that it is even possible to be religious and flamboyant at the same time.)

As for the conservative argument, I always enjoy pointing out that until very recently it was conservatives who were most concerned with the details of masculine appearance. Until the democratic era, aristocrats in most European countries displayed their status through clothing which was so flamboyant that it looks ridiculous to modern eyes. Most European countries had "sumptuary laws" until at least the eighteenth century, which forbade the wearing of luxurious fabrics, and even certain colours, by commoners (that is, by all of us – the vast bulk of the population). The masculine display of beauty represented as deep a conservatism as ever existed.

The most famous dandy in British history, George "Beau" Brummell (1778–1840), was in fact anti-flamboyant: his contribution to received ideas about men's dress was to insist on simplicity and modesty. Virginia Woolf wrote of him:

Everybody looked overdressed, or badly dressed – some, indeed, looked positively dirty – beside him. His clothes seemed to melt into each other with the perfection of their cut and the quiet harmony of their colour. Without a single point of emphasis everything was distinguished. . . . He was the personification of freshness and cleanliness and order. . . . That "certain exquisite propriety" which Lord Byron remarked in his dress stamped his whole being, and made him appear cool, refined and debonair among the gentlemen who talked only of sport, which Brummell detested, and smelt of the stable, which Brummell never visited.

Beau Brummell

His shirts were plain white linen. His breeches were plain, although they did fit very snugly, evidence of their superior tailoring. In the day he would wear them with riding boots and a riding coat, in the evening with silk stockings and pumps. A dandy could not wear embroidery on his coat. Brummell shunned perfume, insisting on "country washing."

In fact most of his dress was a variation on what had until then been thought of as country dressing, and in this his modesty was actually part of a larger social revolution. In the early nineteenth century, democracy was erupting in bloody revolutions everywhere. France had been in disarray from 1789 to 1801, during which dressing like a fop was actually life endangering. (Even the English government put a tax on hair-powder in 1795, so it was almost immediately abandoned as a fashion by young men.) France then had two more revolutions, in 1830 and 1848, which served as grisly warnings to the *anciens régimes* still hoping to keep their heads in the rest of Europe. Aristocracies were decidedly out of fashion. The wealthy middle class was in the ascendant; it began to seem more respectable, less decadent – and thus decidedly safer – to look like a bourgeois rather than a duke. English dress – country dress – became the official uniform even of French men after 1800.

Even Beau Brummell's favoured outfit of tight breeches and fine hose had disappeared from everyday life by around 1840. It is still worn in certain European royal courts on special occasions, as it has come to signify aristocratic associations.

It was at this time that the dark suit, white shirt, and dark tie first approached the status of uniform for men of all classes. It has evolved in only minor ways since then.

King Louis-Philippe of France (r. 1830–1848) became known as *le roi bourgeois* because of his insistence on wearing the sober black suit of the businessman. He provoked ridicule in the French press by making a public appearance with an umbrella under his arm, looking more like a businessman than a king. The ridicule was short-lived: from this moment on, dandyism lost its cachet. Power and status were no longer signalled by ostentatious display. The great era of male uniformity had begun.

There were a couple of exceptions to this set of values. The most significant is the military. Here, the toughest warriors have always been got up like peacocks, plumed and feathered and shiny with gold braid. This is the area of greatest paradox – for isn't this kind of colourful and meticulously groomed display supposed to be feminine?

Try telling that to an officer in Wellington's cavalry, with his vast bearskin hat and miles of intricate lanyard, his supertight breeches and little cape. Or to the Swiss Guard, the oldest military force in the world, with their Harlequin-striped pantaloons. These are not sissies.

It wasn't until the First World War that camouflage became actively valued by armed forces in Europe. The idea of dressing to disappear would have been thought cowardly by nineteenth-century soldiers – and also feminine. Concealment, disguise, manipulating the body's silhouette – all constitute a kind of false advertising, and was that not a woman's specialty?

Camouflage was and still is restricted to the battlefield. Right through the twentieth century, military dress uniforms were far flashier, far more fussy and beribboned than their civilian counterparts. The English novelist Simon Raven describes, in a memoir, a memorial church service just after the end of the Second World War, in which all the servicemen present are decked out in their dress uniforms:

While all of us were wearing scruffy grey flannels and patched tweed jackets, the champions of England were hung about with every colour and device. . . . There were the black and gold hats of the guardsmen, the dark-green side-caps of the rifles, kilts swaying from the hips of the highlanders, and ball buttons sprayed all over the horse artillerymen; there were macabre facings and curiously knotted lanyards; there were even the occasional boots and spurs, though these were frowned on in 1945 because of Fascist associations. . . . I myself had a place in the Sixth Form block which commanded a good view of the visitors, and I could see that the magnificent officers were openly preening themselves.

My point is that although one might think these peacock warriors a little silly, no one would think them feminine. There is nothing unmanly about a proud and meticulous appearance.

Here, of course, my detractors from the left are crowing in satisfaction. Yes, exactly, they are saying, and is the vain and overdressed warrior really a valuable model for contemporary man? Do we really want to dress like imperialist murderers?

The sensitive socialist opposition to refinement and elegance in dress was at its most powerful in the 1960s and 70s. A strange thing happened to men's appearances in the Western world some time around the middle of the 1960s. As part of the general social revolution of the era, the natural was embraced over the artificial. One might as well put these words in quotation marks, as they are so vague and inaccurate and paradoxical as to be almost meaningless, but we all follow the general idea: natural man did not attempt to restrain the physical processes. He let his hair grow on his face and head; he did not restrict his body with supposedly uncomfortable clothing such as shoes and ties; his clothes were loose and rough. Rough was manly and egalitarian; smooth was fake and old-fashioned.

These beliefs are still widely held in rural areas and among baby boomers. You read middle-aged newspaper columnists and hear talk-radio hosts snickering at the idea of male grooming: they bring up the laughable term "metrosexual"; they paint a caricature of a preening sissy who spends his time

"As part of the general SOCIAL REVOLUTION of the 1960s, the NATURAL was embraced over the ARTIFICIAL."

being manicured and pedicured and waxed, who sits on the phone with his friends arguing the merits of hair products. Again, recognize that women are just as disconcerted by these supposedly contemporary practices as men are: it is female newspaper columnists in provincial papers who are going to be the most scornful about men who wear cologne and "smell like girls."

This idea of manliness is, in historical terms, highly unusual and also very short-lived. The hysterical radio hosts are threatened by the twenty-year-old men they see dashing by on skateboards with dyed and gelled hair, and possibly wearing cologne. Younger men's sexuality is not so easily threatened. Sophistication, and expression through appearance, are back in style.

To illustrate this, I would like you to consider quiche. A young friend who is not a native speaker of English once asked me rather shyly what was the understood meaning of the word *quiche*. She knew what a quiche was: a French tart made with eggs. She had even eaten quiche. But in books she had read it seemed to have a strange significance: it seemed to connote weakness or even homosexuality. Why was this? As far as she knew it was a rather rugged dish, indeed a peasant dish.

So I painstakingly explained one of those long-forgotten American cultural tropes that makes one embarrassed now. There was a time, I explained, in the late 1970s and early 1980s, when North America was going through a kind of cultural adolescence, and the idea of subtlety and sophistication and all things European were becoming popular in large cities. This was frightening to people outside large cities. For example, for the first time, the English pop groups who appeared in American magazines had short hair, evidence that they rejected the essentially manly and patriotic and democratic values of rock and roll. It was upsetting that some people on this side of the Atlantic would embrace their music; it seemed snotty.

It was also upsetting that some people – the same kind of people, probably – became interested at the same time in eating food that wasn't very heavy and fatty. Eating french fries every day, they said, was bad for your heart. This also seemed, to many North Americans, to be an insidious attack on respectable values. There were jokes about "nouvelle cuisine," a style of cooking with lighter sauces, a rip-off that had you paying twenty bucks for a sliver of salmon and a sprig of parsley – common-sense folk could see through such pretension, as they could see through the sham of modern art.

It was hard to explain to my friend the idea that any kind of pie, with a crust made with lard, could have qualified as diet food, but I tried to get her to understand that as an alternative to a burger and fries it probably did. The fact that quiche was French likely made it seem doubly silly to many.

The joke was concretized in the 1982 book *Real Men Don't Eat Quiche*, by Bruce Feirstein and Lee

Lorenz, which listed all the aspects of civilization that were emasculating: any kind of sensitivity, any kind of self-expression, any interest in the aesthetic. The book was self-satirizing – its intent was to mock the extremism of its fears – but it was nevertheless extremely popular among people for whom it was not entirely a joke. It was, I remember, a popular gift book for dads at the time.

I listed for my friend the other associated terms that were humorously used by the media at the time – fern bar (remember that?), wine bar, spritzer, aerobics, Chardonnay, brie, yuppie – to signal pretension, effeteness, and a kind of California flakiness. People who ordered spritzers in fern bars were posers. In other words, the term "quiche-eater" once meant pretty much what "metrosexual" does now. But it doesn't any more, and many restaurants and bars are furnished with cut flowers and plants, and drinking wine instead of beer doesn't seem quite as gay any more, and most middle-class people would qualify as yuppies, so we don't use the word.

That quiche has lost its negative connotations indicates the culture has changed. It is a little more sophisticated. Gradually, we push through our fears and widen our interests to include foreign food and music and even, occasionally, books. Now nineteen-year-old tough guys shave their body hair. Quiche doesn't worry anybody: it has become just a dull egg tart again.

There are still barriers to cross, as the scorn over "metrosexual" indicates. The next terrifying barrier is the male use of moisturizers, contemplation of which still induces hoots of hysterical giggles among people of a certain age. This will fade.

That period of insecurity, and the triumph of the natural, were a historical blip. Outside those dark twenty-odd years in the middle of the last century, sophistication was always masculine. Even in the 1950s, it was considered manly to be well-groomed. Consider Cary Grant, the romantic hero of 1950s Hollywood. He was clean-shaven and wore elegant suits; he knew about what wine to drink with fish and how to mix a martini. Nor is there anything new about pampering: the ritual of the hot shave in a barbershop was a deeply masculine convention right into the 1970s.

More importantly, the privileging of the natural over the artificial is philosophically unjustified. It leads to repressive thinking. For there is nothing inherently morally impure about the artificial. Art and artifice come from the same root – *ars*, *artis*; skill, practice. Skill is a particularly human value. Art is a uniquely human activity. All art is artificial.

We always have an urge to humanize the natural, to stylize and artificialize. Think of tattoos, the imposition of art on the untamed flesh, or tribal scarring, which marks the transition from mere raw flesh to part of civilized being, member of society. It's an old urge.

"There is nothing NEW about PAMPERING: the ritual of the HOT SHAVE in a BARBERSHOP was a deeply MASCULINE convention RIGHT into the 1970s."

Society is fun. The parties are good and the debates are complex. I would no more return to the natural than I would give up Shostakovich and Brahms and the Louvre.

All right. Let's move on to the thornier issue of social class. For are we not, in proposing a set of rules, a system of values, enshrining privilege itself?

It is true that men's clothing relies much more heavily on tradition and convention than it does on fashion, and that these conventions vary among social classes, so as to be actual indicators of social class. Knowledge of these indicators serves to include and to exclude. The people who are aware of very old conventions of men's dress, and particularly of dress-up – suits and ties, military uniforms, formal wear – tend to have come from more privileged backgrounds.

Winston has a sentimental attachment to his beat-up old Timex

This is a quite understandably an upsetting topic in a democratic society which claims to be class-free, so I have to provide a few caveats here. I am an egalitarian. In discussing class differences, I do not propose to reinforce them. It is a wonderful thing that this society attempts to be, or sees itself as, class-free. Would that it really were.

The sad thing is, it's not. The people who are most aware of social class are the privileged. This is how privilege works: it is a secret.

Note that when I say class I do not mean money. Many people have money. Money is very common on this prosperous continent.

Imagine watching a very wealthy salesman pull up outside a flashy new martini bar downtown, in his new convertible Porsche sports car. It is bright yellow. He has a very tanned, very blonde woman with him with expensive breasts. Let's call him Derek. He wears a Rolex, and a gold bracelet on the other arm. And a cream linen suit that cost $3,000. He is tanned too, because he has just come back from a week in Palm Springs. We watch him air-kiss the model standing at the velvet ropes and disappear into the scented, ivory-walled sanctum of pleasure, and we say that because he belongs to this tiny percentile of similarly privileged people, he represents the upper class. This is the media definition of class: it can be quantified.

The genuinely privileged guy inside this bar – let's call him Winston – has been dragged here by some new clients. He doesn't feel comfortable. He is wearing a beat-up old Timex. He has a sentimental attachment to it; it was his dad's. He has not travelled anywhere recently, because he has only fifteen hundred dollars in the bank right now (Derek, on the other hand, has $2.1 million, and that's just what's liquid).

But Winston's family has $400 million. (Or had, actually: his father lost most of it. But only after sending Winston to some strangely violent private schools.) That's why he doesn't worry about watches or Palm Springs much. He has become very interested in Proust, lately, and has been brushing up on his French in an effort to read it in the original.

Derek wears a Rolex and a cream linen suit

Winston may find Derek fascinating and even intimidating. But he would not describe him as upper class. Winston would not even describe himself as upper class, that stratum being strictly speaking a European concept, only applicable to actual aristocrats; that is, people with a title. Even very established families in England call themselves "upper-middle class" if they don't have a title. In North America, lacking titles of any kind, our very top stratum is in effect only upper-middle class. Winston would not call Derek even that. He would call him a successful businessman. But he would not have this conversation with anyone; it would be impolite.

Class is something inherited (often, but not always, along with money), or acquired through elite education (which usually also costs money). Class can build itself up as a result of money – but usually only after several generations and serious efforts at assimilation. Social class is reflected and stored in social habits that are dependent on money, but do not come solely from the money itself. It is reflected by certain kinds of education, certain modes of speech (this is where the most insidious shibboleths are preserved), and aesthetic choices, including, particularly, dress.

These indicators are worthy of an entire book (and I can recommend one – Paul Fussell's admirably dispassionate *Class*). So I can only skim the surface of those that do not belong to the sartorial domain. But the linguistic and the sartorial indicators often go hand in hand. You do not know, for example, that people of a certain privileged class do not easily use the word *tuxedo* unless you belong to that class yourself. The majority of the world – clothing manufacturers and salesmen included – use the word.

The same goes for *limousine* and *chauffeur* – the people who are most likely to be wearing tuxedos in limousines driven by chauffeurs are in fact the least likely to use those words. (They will say they are wearing *dinner jackets* in *cars* driven by *drivers*.) Again, the secret codes exist for entirely pernicious reasons: they identify members of the club, like secret handshakes, *only to each other.*

There are many such class codes in the arcana of men's clothing. Take shoelaces. As in questions of how-many-buttons or which-knot-to-tie, a man of a certain social class believes that there is a correct way and an incorrect way to lace your shoes. (Later in this book, I will show you the "correct" way.) In this context, all "correct" means is a signifier of breeding, of "gentlemanliness," recognized only by other "gentlemen."

Yes, these are outmoded, if not nasty and dangerous, concepts. Like many of these codes, the lacing has a military origin: it is often said that the horizontal laces are easier to slit with a knife in an emergency, if your shoe must be removed rapidly. This association with action and danger makes men feel more manly. But the practical function is utterly irrelevant to a lawyer in a boardroom. The

"THERE are many CLASS CODES in the ARCANA of men's clothing. Take SHOELACES."

horizontal lace is now a mere rule, a symbol of military lineage.

All such rules – such arcane conventions as closing the top two, but not the bottom, buttons of a jacket, or ensuring a dimple in your tie, or not removing your jacket in a restaurant, or not wearing brogues with a dinner jacket, or wearing a tie at all – serve no practical function. Sure, they once did. Ties, for example, evolved from knotted scarves, which served to keep the collar closed and the neck warm. But in an age of Velcro, we no longer need $150 pieces of printed Italian silk to keep the breeze out. And yet the conventions remain, serving largely as a barrier against the free social mobility of those with the misfortune to have been born at any distance from country clubs and hidebound tailors. Why, then, do I – in a supposedly class-free society – persist in promoting a catechism of exclusionary practices?

I have no interest in perpetuating exclusion. My hope is that my explanation of these codes will have exactly the opposite effect: to open up the country club to all, by revealing the secret codes of the initiates.

One could argue that even in merely describing class practices one helps to promote them. I disagree. Class will be around for a long time to come, whether I talk about shoelaces or not, and it will remain a powerful force in society. It is better to understand it – and use it, cynically perhaps (why not?), to one's advantage.

(As an aside, I should explain that I find both Winston and Derek fascinating, and feel, like most people, that neither of them describes me. Certain things are attractive about each. I want to drive Derek's car, no question – I might not get it in yellow. And I think I might prefer Derek's dangerous girlfriend to Winston's somewhat brittle wife – there are only so many fundraisers I can attend. But I don't want that Rolex. A part of me still admires that beat-up old Timex.)

It is also important to explain, to my socialist opposition, that I am not insisting on great expenditure. Indeed, this book is specifically directed at those who are just beginning to assemble their grown-up wardrobes, and I am assuming that they are not yet wealthy. (I hope to help them become so.) Throughout, I will include tips on cheaper alternatives to the ideal.

I myself don't value money all that much, which is why I have been able to tolerate living as a freelance writer for fifteen years, on a very small income by urban standards. I have been able to afford very few of the clothes I have written about. I choose a few pieces very carefully, I match them with cheaper items and vintage pieces. It is possible to look good on very little. It's just a matter of paying attention and thinking about it.

And, as my example of Winston and Derek demonstrates, it is rarely desirable to look as if one is wearing expensive clothes. The second-hand dinner jacket often looks much more distinguished than the trendy new one.

I once read an interview with an exclusive and prohibitively expensive Savile Row tailor, who said, "If someone approaches one of our clients and says, that's a natty suit you're wearing, we have not done our job well." He wants people to notice the client, not the suit. He knows a "gentleman's" values.

I would also point out to the socialists that fashion – that is, a set of changing rules, as opposed to convention – is actually an egalitarian force. Conservatives hate fashion even more than you do. Fashion seeks to do away with tradition, and with it all the special knowledge required to enter the most powerful circles.

Fashion influences men's clothing far more slowly than it does women's. But it does. Those wacky runway shows you see sometimes on TV, with androgynous male models slumping along in skirts and sandals or with flowers in their hair – those trends actually do trickle down to Fit-Rite Clothiers on your town's main street, in some diluted form, five years later. The rules – the old rules, the class-determined conventions – do change. And fashion is, as North America grows more sophisticated and European, gradually becoming more powerful, gradually more accepted by the old guard. Fashion

"FASHION seeks to do away with TRADITION, and with it all the SPECIAL knowledge REQUIRED to enter the most POWERFUL circles."

– the idea of clothing as artistic palette, rather than as uniform – has a greater and greater impact on men's attire. Rules about matching shoes with suits, for example, have greatly relaxed over the past ten years, even in conservative circles. High-fashion designers and, in particular, stylists – the people who dress the models for photos – have little respect for rules.

Let me give an example of how this works. I was arranging a photo shoot for a newspaper feature on shirts and ties. We had borrowed a $2,700 Gianluca Isaia suit for the shoot, and it had arrived with its basting still sewn in. (The basting is the white thread over certain seams that is removed once alterations are done.) The stylist, who like all stylists was wildly glamorous, an unfathomably young woman in long skirt, clingy top, puffy runners, was taken with the idea of shooting the suit with the basting still in. I, bound by rules, was horrified. She thought it looked kind of cool: deconstructed, perhaps, or just ironic.

This is how massive trends are born. It only takes one stylist. Sure enough, a few weeks later I saw some hip black suits in a downtown designer's window with big white stitching on the shoulders and cuffs as a reference to tailor's basting.

This is why conservatives loathe fashion: it opens the game to twenty-five-year-old female stylists. Which makes it a pleasant game to be in.

I still cannot help lacing my shoes in exactly the same way my father taught me, in case I run into someone who knows the pointless and archaic rules, and I am going to go on telling you these rules. In case you want to know.

And you might want to know, you really might. It is useful to know rules, particularly if you are new to this whole game and don't trust your own taste. Men are not brought up to cultivate their aesthetic side. Rules are men's friends: they can substitute for taste.

If you are proud of your taste, know a great deal about fashion, *and* know the rules and are not afraid to break them, then you will not need to read this book. You are already in the Advanced Class – and the point of this book is to get you into that class, to develop your taste to the degree that you no longer need rules.

I myself am interested in both fashion and convention, and I enjoy their uneasy balance, the tension between them. I have very particular views on when to be daring and when to be cautious. I am interested in cynical self-advancement and in very serious self-expression through how I dress. These are complex and endlessly fascinating topics.

I don't recommend an instant following of every new trend. Some fashions are simply ugly. Alexander Pope came up with a useful adage regarding trendiness: "Be not the first by whom the new are tried/ Nor yet the last to lay the old aside."

This brings up the old distinction between fashion and style: fashion is what is out there for

"It is USEFUL to know RULES, particularly if you are NEW to this whole GAME and don't TRUST your own TASTE."

you to choose from; style is what you choose. It is common for aesthetic experts to proclaim at this point that style is all and fashion is not worth bothering about; style relies on what is timeless and classic, blah, blah. Very safe advice, but also very conservative. And a little dishonest. You do have to follow fashion, or at least be aware of what is in and out, to be stylish. The line between them is a blurry one at best. There is no such thing as timeless fashion – if there were, we would still be wearing togas. Those who claim to avoid fashion are usually simply in the grip of an older fashion. When your dad encourages you to check out the sale at Fit-Rite Clothiers in your hometown, where there are "good, solid, classic" suits which "never go out of style," he is in denial. He is fooling himself and trying to fool you. Those suits are going to look perfectly acceptable, but they are not going to make you feel sexy and cool. Their minor, almost imperceptible differences from the ones in downtown stores in big cities – their button stance, the size of the armholes, the length of the jacket – make a difference to the way you will be perceived.

This book is more concerned with convention, and with fashions that seem to be stable, than with the newest fashions, those runway shows with the sarongs and the windsurfing boots or crocheted swimsuits. Those trends – the "forward" end of the business – tend to affect casual wear more than they affect city attire. Furthermore, those who are truly unintimidated by the deep end of men's fashion are in the Advanced Class already, and have no need of me.

It's not that I am opposed to all and every excess. I don't believe that flamboyance – what some would call vulgarity – is always unmanly. The opposite of cool is not vulgar; it is bland. Bland is the enemy of style. The occasional bit of vulgarity can be charming.

No, the enemy is the blight of athletic wear for comfort in mall parking lots and in restaurants; it is bright blue fleece jogging jackets and kayaking sandals, pleated khaki shorts and T-shirts with faded concert advertisements on them.

I am about to offer you some alternatives. If you must feel altruistic about everything you do, think of your appearance as a gift to others. A pleasant aspect shows respect for people around you. Physically attractive people are pleasant to be around, just as beautiful buildings are pleasant to live in, and warm rooms are preferable to cold. You are not a superficial man: you are making the world a more beautiful place. This is what art is about, and it is a serious thing to do. It will be, like art, at once pleasurable and intellectual. It will be like Shostakovich.

And we begin at the roots of your appearance, the fundament on which your whole style will be built: your feet.

CHAPTER ONE

SHOES

Fashion is only the attempt to realize Art
in living forms and social intercourse.
— OLIVER WENDELL HOLMES

An experienced society columnist once summed up her whole method of placing people in the social hierarchy by telling me, "It's all in the shoes."

Nowhere is your taste and social background so neatly summarized as in your choice of shoe. It is the single most important part of your image, the root from which your projected self grows. Large numbers of single women judge prospective male partners rapidly and solely by looking at their feet.

Shoes are the only item of clothing on which you really must spend a great deal of money. It is not really important for the rest of your ensemble. An inexpensive but modishly cut suit can fool TV cameras and fashion journalists alike; a Le Château shirt is perfectly hip during its six-month lifespan; a twenty-dollar tie from Wal-Mart is still pure silk. But cheap shoes always look bad. Cheap shoes will also wear out. Good shoes can be resoled almost infinitely and will obviate shoe-buying for ten years. From a purely financial standpoint, you cannot afford cheap shoes.

To know quality you must be aware of technical specifications. There is a scene in Don DeLillo's novel *Underworld* in which a Jesuit intellectual attempts to educate a delinquent pupil by teaching him the names for all the parts of the shoe: **sole, heel, lace, tongue, cuff** (the strip of leather around the top edge), **quarter** (the rear sides), **counter** (the strip of leather over the heel, also called the back-stay), **welt** (the leather base between the upper and the sole), **vamp** (the front area over the instep), **eyelet, grommet** (the metal rings that reinforce the eyelets), **aglet** (the plastic sheath at the end of the lace). And the wooden form that the cobbler makes shoes on is called a **last** (leading to the old joke about shoemaking: the last comes first). The Jesuit's contention is that "everyday things represent the most overlooked knowledge."

For our purposes, the point is not only that great literature is obsessed with fashion (something repeatedly demonstrated in these pages), but also that you cannot know a thing until you have words for it. I think that the words *welt* and *sole* are the most overlooked "everyday knowledge" in fashion.

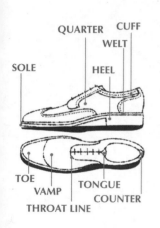

QUARTER CUFF
WELT
SOLE HEEL

TOE
VAMP TONGUE
COUNTER
THROAT LINE

Anatomy of the shoe

In the first half of the twentieth century, a fine, light shoe was probably Italian-made, and therefore evidence of wealth and sophisticated taste. Many elegant Italian shoes were constructed without a welt – that is, with the uppers stitched directly to the leather sole, with no intervening stiffener. Heavily welted English shoes, made for walking in cold climates, were, in the 1950s, the mark of the plodding Anglo-Saxon in a baggy suit; Europeans had trimmer silhouettes and lighter feet.

This is no longer the case. Mass-produced footwear has been emulating the narrow, slipper-like Italian style since the seventies. Thin-soled shoes have become indicators of cheap production techniques (most uppers are now glued, rather than stitched, to the welt) and connoters of discount malls and oily moustaches. A thick leather sole and leather welt will give you authority, will cost you more, and will last forever.

Soles wear out long before uppers do. One way of ensuring your sole's longevity is to take your new shoes to your cobbler (you have a cobbler, don't you?) the day after you buy them and have him install a thin **protective rubber sole** over the leather *before* the original sole wears out. This procedure will cost you about twenty dollars. Make sure the rubber layer is not too thick, and it will be invisible. It will give you greater traction. And when it wears out, you spend another twenty dollars rather than buying a new pair of shoes.

"A THICK leather sole and LEATHER WELT will give you AUTHORITY, will cost you MORE, and will last FOREVER."

Guys with a lot of money won't need or want to do this – in wealthy circles, this practice is seen to be a little parsimonious, and it is certainly more elegant to have a plain leather sole than one with a rubber coating, no matter how thin. Wealthy guys may worry that when they sit and cross their legs, their rubber protective sole will become visible and make them look like penny-pinching students. I still insist that if your cobbler does it right, the rubber layer will be completely unnoticeable from above. And if people are staring at the soles of your feet when you sit down, they are looking rather determinedly to find fault somewhere, so let them. The practice of resoling good shoes has saved me hundreds of dollars – I am currently still wearing, with formal wear, a pair of very plain black leather oxfords with a toecap (a line of stitching across the toe), which I bought from the Canadian firm Dacks in 1987, making them, at the time of this writing, eighteen years old.

Note that *the original sole, in a pair of dress shoes*, must *be leather*. In a casual outfit, for bars and parties and shopping, you may wear Dr. Martens or Blundstones or police boots or heavily lugged streetwear boots from techno-playing East Village stores. But a business suit is capsized by a comfy pair of rubber-soled shoes, no matter how shiny the leather uppers. Rockports – the popular sport shoes that disguise themselves as dress shoes with leather uppers in brogue styles – are the worst blight to

"A BUSINESS suit is CAPSIZED by a comfy pair of RUBBER-SOLED shoes, no matter how SHINY the leather UPPERS."

hit office-wear conventions. (Okay, second perhaps to casual Fridays.) Your Rockports aren't fooling anyone: they still look like sneakers to me.

There is also a new style of faux leather sole – a sole that is half leather, with rubber patches in the centre and leather around the edges, so that it looks to be all leather when viewed from above. These look civilized, and are often quite expensive, but your cobbler cannot affix the aforementioned protective layer to them. This is fine if your financial situation allows you to replace your shoes once every two years or so.

Which with What – Shoe Styles

Very conservative thinking has it like this: for a suit and tie, black lace-up **oxfords** only. No options. Even **brogues**, the heavy walking shoes decorated with strips of hole-punched ("tooled") leather – also called "**wingtips**," because the decorative layer of leather on top of the toe often comes to a point – were once thought to be too casual for a city suit and more appropriate for tweeds and other country wear. (Note that a brogue, by coincidence, also means a heavy rural accent.) But now brogues, black or burgundy, are considered just as serious a suit foundation as any plain shoe. (Again, as long as they have a grown-up leather sole.)

Oxford (left) and brogue shoes

"Long wingtips" are so called because the sides of the toecap – the part that makes the wingtip design – extend right back to meet at the backstay.

Long and short wingtips

"Short wings" means that the toecap curves downward at the sides and vanishes into the welt.

There are several hybrids of brogues and oxfords. If the decorative tooled leather runs across the toe in a straight line, that is, without coming to a "wingtip" point, it is called a half-brogue. But this is truly useless information. The important thing to know is that the more decoration there is on a shoe, the less formal it is. For example, some shoes have a texture known as "pebbled" – the leather looks slightly bumpy or wrinkled. Nothing wrong with this, but I picture it more with a sports jacket and flannel trousers than with a severe pinstriped business suit. Highly ceremonial occasions demand very sleek, unadorned leather.

Note too that the way the flaps that hold the eyelets are sewn into the rest of the upper indicates a hierarchy of dressiness. "**Closed**" lacing means that the two sides of the upper that are drawn together by the laces are sewn *under* the rest of the upper. The tongue is a separate piece which is also sewn onto the underside of the vamp. "**Open**" lacing means that the two flaps are sewn *onto the top* of the upper. The tongue is just an extension of the vamp. Shoes with open lacing are sometimes called **Bluchers** in Britain, apparently because the Prussian field marshal Blucher (who was Wellington's highly successful ally at Waterloo) issued his troops with boots in a similar style. They are also sometimes called **Derbys**.

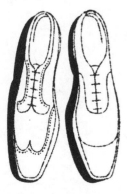

Closed lacing (right) versus open

Again, it is of no practical value whatsoever to know these terms, which are increasingly forgotten by the industry anyway, but I cannot help revelling in the words as much as in the objects. If you must look at this in practical terms, know that the only lesson here is closed lacing means a more formal shoe.

Shoes with open lacing will often have metal **grommets** placed in the eyelets. This creates a rugged outdoorsy or industrial look which may be appropriate for corduroy trousers and a tweed jacket, but not for a business suit.

Generally, the rules for pairing shoes with suits have relaxed greatly. **Slip-ons**, for example, can be quite formal-looking these days, as long as they have a high **vamp** (the vamp is the part where the laces are if the shoe has laces – the part that covers the top front of your foot). Low-vamp, moccasin-like loafers still look too much like slippers for wear with a tie. And no one wants to see too much of your socks.

Even buckles, on slip-ons, can look quite sober, as long as they are to one side: loafers with a gleaming snaffle in the centre of the vamp (like the standard Canadian-politician Gucci loafer) are, however, just too casual for a suit (and too plain tacky for anything else).

And finally, let me make this clear: There is no occasion or outfit in civilized society which justifies the wearing of loafers with a leather fringe and a dangling tassel over the vamp. These shoes are an abomination.

> "There is no OCCASION or OUTFIT in civilized society which JUSTIFIES the wearing of LOAFERS with a leather FRINGE and a dangling TASSEL."

The spit and polish method

Traditional military methods provide the best shine. There are all kinds of military tricks for instant results, if you are late for parade and need a quick fix, such as rubbing the inside of a banana peel all over your shoe (not recommended, even in a fix), or slathering a heavy layer of wax on the shoe and then melting it with a match held close (danger-ous: it's easy to burn the leather). The only reliable shine is the most labour-intensive one: it's the old spit and polish method. This shine builds over weeks of meticulous repe-tition. It requires old-fashioned wax polish, available in cute little tins at any grocery store (Kiwi brand is still the best). You take a soft shoe cloth, wrap it around your finger, and use it to smear on a generous amount of polish. Oh no! It looks as if you've ruined it – your shoe has gone all dull! ☞

A recent trend among fashion-forward designers has been to pair shiny, lace-up **ankle boots** with dark suits. This turn-of-the-century look I find romantic. It is for the daring only, and not appro-priate for the more conservative boardrooms of the financial or political world.

A **"Chelsea boot"** is a slip-on ankle boot (some-times also called Beatle boots, for obvious reasons). Its current incarnations tend to have blunt toes, rather than the pointy toes of their Carnaby Street forebears (more on the blunt/pointy conundrum in a moment); both are appropriate with casual suits – that is, suits worn without ties – for fashionable rather than conservative environments.

The shape of men's shoes changes with fashion. These changes are even more noticeable than those in suits and shirts. As I write this, the most fashion-conscious have just shifted their loyalties *en masse* from wide square toes to narrower shoes that almost look pointy (indeed, the current style resem-bles the "winkle-pickers" of the mod era). The new pointy shoes still have slightly blunted toes – if you stand the shoe upright on its backstay, you can balance a quarter on the toe.

Variations in stitching are also increasingly pop-ular: fashionable shoes often have a "split toe"; that is, a visible line of stitching joining the two sides of the upper, visible on the toe. Or you will find two seams running down the vamp, right to the sole. All of these can be acceptable for dressy suits, but use your judgment, because the stitching can be excessive.

And remember that these styles are ephemeral. You can never go wrong with a classic round-toed oxford, either with a toecap or without, or with classic brogues.

Colours

There were once strict rules for matching the colour of your shoe with the colour of your suit, but these are disappearing as well. I have caused a veritable firestorm of outrage by writing in a newspaper that I accepted the wearing of brown shoes with charcoal or navy suits. This was once strictly taboo in class-conscious circles; brown shoes with a dark suit were, in my father's day, a sign of an outsider, like the wearing of a pre-tied bow tie or clip-on suspenders. My father tolerates brown shoes only with a sports jacket – particularly with a tweed jacket, which demands them.

But like the old adage that red wine is for meat and white for fish, the injunction that brown shoes are casual is outdated. Indeed, a man pairing a navy suit with a pair of brown suede oxfords is quietly displaying his confidence and his aestheticism, which I admire. **Burgundy** or **oxblood** (which is slightly darker; also called **cordovan**, from a kind of expensive leather) is a particularly versatile colour with suits, matching light grey, dark grey, or beige. These combinations will make you look modern and possibly Italian.

No fear; this is only the beginning. You spit – only a little bit – on the mess you've made and then start rubbing in tiny circles. This is crucial: tiny circles, not wide swaths. You go over and over the circles you've just made until a shine starts to come up. If it doesn't, spit a little bit more. You will get to learn, with practice, what exact ratio of spit to polish will bring up the best gloss. If you do it with enough patience, you will not need to brush off excess polish afterward. You might use an even finer shoe rag – a woman's nylon is particularly effective here – to buff when you are finished. The process takes experimentation, failure, frustration. It takes layer after fine layer, applied week after week. But soon – sooner than you know it – your shoes will be impervious to even salted slush, at least for the duration of the walk between the taxi and the red carpet. ✒

Lacing

By the time you have graduated from elementary school you should know that you don't lace your dress shoes in a simple criss-cross pattern. A gentleman knows that his laces should be neatly parallel. Now, there are different methods for achieving this, and some steamy debate over which is the most elegant or practical. I have included some handy diagrams here so that you can analyze the problem and make your own decisions.

The first, the system we might call the Underweb, provides the most flexible tightening ability, but does rely on some messy underpinning. We want to cut down on all the visible strings under your neat row of parallel lines.

The second, which we will baptize the Secret Web, has fewer visible underpinnings, but is a bitch to tighten.

The third, which we shall call the Ballroom, is the most sleek and ☞

I would, however, warn against very light-coloured leather shoes: grey or tan or white. They always look cheap, no matter how expensive they are.

Bright colours are fine for very casual shoes such as sneakers or running shoes, meant for wearing with shorts or jeans and skateboarding in. If we are not talking about suits and ties, then you don't need my advice: go nuts.

Suede shoes can be beautiful with sports jackets of all colours. Suede shoes should be brown; they are too informal for black.

A particular kind of moulded rubber sole – a sole that looks organic, like an approximation of the foot itself, and that curls up at the front and back to become particularly visible – became popular in the 1990s and is still influencing fashion-forward styles even in dress shoes. This was the great contribution to the history of masculine footwear from the Italian designer Miuccia Prada, and its influence has been far out of proportion to its beauty. For about ten years you couldn't see an architect or curator walking a loft floor without glimpsing the telltale red heel dot of the Prada label; it was the mark of downtown consciousness. It was probably popular because the curvy sole looked both futuristic and athletic, like something to keep your feet stuck on a wet windsurfing board. I have always been baffled by the success of the Prada sole design and have long wished it a speedy obsolescence.

My wish is coming true, as the Prada sole has

been copied by so many low-end casual shoe manufacturers that it is now a staple of the discount racks at mall outlets.

Stick with sober flat soles and you will avoid this association.

Shoes with Formal Wear

For black or white tie, ancient wisdom demands **patent leather** oxfords (in Britain) or **court pumps** (in America). Patent leather is that treated leather that looks as shiny as plastic. It doesn't need polishing. Court pumps are those very low-vamp loafers with a little grosgrain silk bow just above the toe.

Both demands are outdated. Patent leather is great if you can afford a special pair of shoes for your dinner jacket. But to court pumps I wish a curt good riddance, as they always looked frilly and ridiculous. Nowadays a simple black leather oxford will match both black and white tie, as long as it is polished to a high gloss.

I still would avoid brogues, however, with black tie. Remember that the more elaborately patterned or stitched the shoe, the less slick and therefore less formal it is.

I don't need to tell you, by this point, that loafers with little tassels, indeed loafers of any kind, or any shoes with rubber soles, are embarrassingly wrong with black tie.

And if you think it's amusing to break the rules of formal dressing by matching a dinner jacket with

elegant of all, but is hugely impractical when it comes to tightening your shoe. Furthermore, it is only practicable on shoes with a certain number of eyelets. Try it with a five-eyelet shoe, and you will be backed into a deadly end-game with no option but to have two ends emerging from the same hole. It works with four eyelets, however. ๖

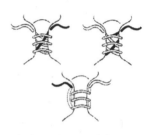

(clockwise from top left)
The Secret Web, the
Underweb, the *Ballroom*

canvas tennis shoes, then you should stop reading immediately. You are angry about something, and want to be talking about politics instead.

Sandals

This is possibly the most treacherous terrain for the male foot. It is hot; you are bound for a boardwalk or ice-cream café; you are wearing shorts . . . a sandal comes to mind. And yet, and yet . . . there is something inherently squirm-making, some monster of humiliation from childhood that comes on us as we consider all the delicate and dainty or geriatric variations on woven leather in the window of Fit-Rite Clothiers.

It is fear of unmanliness, fear of childhood or perhaps of old age, that drives so many men to the athletic sandal, to the kayaking shoe made of recycled rubber, with its bright nylon straps and plastic snaps and Velcro closures. So sporty, so environmentally conscious, so save-the-rain-forest. Or to the super-industrial Caterpillar-style running-shoe sandal, with its foam running-shoe sole, its black-and-yellow straps like air-intake warnings – it looks like a cross between a parachute harness and a helicopter engine. The fact that these things were originally designed for maximum practicality while kayaking or rafting (they don't slip or rot in water) is precisely what makes them inappropriate for city wear, and precisely what makes them so popular. Men who wear Tevas or Cats to the mall on a

Saturday morning are the same men who drive pumped-up four-wheel drive vehicles up and down the seamlessly paved expressways; they are the same men who wear pilots' or scuba-divers' watches (bristling with dials and buttons, accurate to three hundred metres underwater, complete with compass and GPS) to air-conditioned boardrooms.

We all like to think we're Action Man. We like to think we're rugged and practical, prepared to burst, at a moment's notice, out of our gabardine suits and rappel down the side of the building. And we're also hopelessly childish when it comes to high-tech stuff. If a new fabric is announced by Dupont to resist gamma rays while in zero-gravity spacewalk, we *must* buy something made of it, *right away* (for mowing the lawn).

I understand this attraction. But the Mountain Equipment Co-op aesthetic is just too goofy to be tolerated in the city (or even in the woods, for that matter). All those bright, cheery nylons are children's colours, and nylon is a nasty, synthetic substance anyway. Moreover, the healthy, formless androgyny of high-tech outdoor wear is sexless, sensuality-free. Teva sandals, comfortable and cool as they may be, are depressing.

So, what to do? Sandals are, I admit, a tricky business. Toes and heels, gnarled and calloused, are not the most attractive parts of the male body. Old-fashioned sandals such as **slides** with two wide straps and a heel strap cry out for a straw hat and a bird-watching guide. Wearing any kind of sandal is courting a certain loss of dignity.

But it is possible to stay cool and stylish: to cover both heel and toe in woven leather straps and let the foot breathe at the same time. I always have a fondness for the classic French schoolboy sandal, known on this continent as the "fisherman." It has a closed heel and toe, decorative holes in the vamp, and a strap and buckle at the top of the vamp. Its cheapest and most casual form is plain black; it has a rubber sole and costs under fifty dollars.

However, men and women alike are justifiably nervous about the fisherman sandal; it is really not very tough-looking, and you must be extremely confident about your masculinity to carry it confidently. There are more grown-up variations on the woven sandal available in expensive shoe stores. I prefer ones with a **closed heel**. (I'm not big on looking at people's heels.)

The most popular contemporary sandal for young men is the plain **slide**, followed closely by the **flip-flop**. The slide is a simple flat sole with one wide band of leather across the instep. They are an extremely naked form of shoe: they are hardly there at all. They also tend to fall off. These are acceptable city wear only if they are leather. Avoid plastic or nylon ones; they look as if they are meant to be worn in the shower.

The flip-flop is even more minimal: it is held on to your foot by the grip between your big toe and

> **"Wearing any kind of SANDAL is courting a certain LOSS of DIGNITY."**

the next toe. At the time of this writing they are everywhere; people under the age of thirty, of both genders, seem to have no problem with flip-flops on men. They associate them with the new breed of hippyish rock star, perhaps, or with a relaxed and confident allure, whereas over-thirties associate them with childhood swimming lessons. Flip-flops – again, leather not plastic – are literally cool, and are increasingly accepted café-terrace wear, but look best on bigger, taller men. Their very lightness is their drawback; they make the smaller man feel childish and insubstantial. Shoes serve an anchoring purpose, they give you a platform from which to battle the world. Flip-flops or slides with jeans may be clothed enough for most, and indeed both can look rakish and manly, but consider flip-flops with shorts or, worse, capris (the long shorts or short trousers that hang to mid-calf): the overall effect is juvenile, flimsy – at worst, dainty.

My favourite form of footwear with shorts is funky suede skateboarding shoes.

This in turn brings up the problem of socks. (Life is complicated!) Bare feet will quickly rot through leather and fabric shoes alike. I don't care. There is nothing you can do about this except dusting your feet with talcum powder before you put on your shoes. And buying new shoes regularly. Under no circumstances can you wear socks of any colour – no, not even white – with shorts. They make you look like a dork. You got this? No socks with shorts. Period.

And no nylon-strap sandals on the feet of anyone who is not actually standing in water, and on anyone who is over sixteen.

Some More No-nos

Cowboy boots. Forget it. They carry with them an inescapable odour of brand-new subdivisions, of airport Holiday Inn lounges . . . in short, of desperation.

Shoe rubbers. We all suffer guilt over this one, largely because of our fathers. We hear their stern, money-saving admonitions, see their dismayed faces, every time we plunge our new leather into the slush. And yet we cringe in embarrassment at the image of respectable men, men with diversified portfolios and frequent-flyer cards, bundled in overcoats, juggling briefcases, bracing themselves against door jambs to tug at the sticky sheaths on their feet. What point is a shiny English brogue if it is covered in dull matte rubber every time you take a stroll down the populous boulevards? This is the male equivalent of the businesswoman's running-shoes-for-the-trip-home, and its time has passed. And yes, there are alternatives. This is what shoe polish is for. It provides a waxy resistance to moisture, and keeps the leather supple. If you polish every day, wipe off salt as soon as it clings (do it in the washroom, with paper towel), store your shoes with cedar shoetrees in them (which absorb moisture and prevent the leather from cracking), and never set them to dry beside a heat source, you can stride through sleet and retain a commanding shine. And throw the rubbers away.

How Many Do I Need?

If you are just starting out with grown-up clothes, you need only two pairs of good shoes.

Even if you don't have to wear a suit to work every day, you will have to own at least one suit for special occasions, and for this one suit you need proper shoes. So start with basic black closed-lacing oxfords. They may have simple stitching forming a toecap, a split toe, or any other line, or not. These will double as your formal shoes for black tie.

Then, for your slightly less dressy outfit of sports jacket and trousers (which is also necessary), you will need one pair of dark brown or burgundy shoes. I suggest heavy burgundy brogues as your second pair. Or, if you see yourself as a fashionable guy, a pair of brown or burgundy ankle boots, lace-up or slip-on.

For very casual summer wear, one pair woven leather sandals or slides. And one pair suede skateboarding shoes for evenings at techno clubs. Get brightly coloured laces in them and your friends will be impressed at your confidence.

I am not addressing practical footwear for specific situations, such as tennis shoes or workboots. You already have those anyway.

I will recommend here, for the Advanced Class only, one flamboyant indulgence that I find to be the

"Start with BASIC black closed-lacing OXFORDS. These will DOUBLE as your formal shoes for BLACK TIE."

sign of the truly sensual and confident: **clogs**. Yes, clogs. The classic Dutch design, with a wooden sole and a plain leather upper, no backstay or ankle strap. They look retro and sensitive; they make people think of Europe. Consider the advantages: clogs add five centimetres in height; they are airy while covering your splintered toenails; they will make women think you are a South American guitarist and fall in love with you.

The perfect clogs are hard to find in North America; you must go to Europe and buy real Dutch ones, which are not expensive. I got a pair in a discount store in Frankfurt for about twenty dollars.

Remember

All this talk of fashionable shoes may distract you from the fact that you can never go wrong, particularly with business dress, with a conservative, expensive, unfashionable pair . . . as long as they have a leather sole. Conservatism in shoes is a sign of breeding, and is much more useful than conservatism in other clothes. Remember that whenever you meet a gossip columnist, she is looking first at your feet.

CHAPTER TWO

SUITS

All the world is not, of course, a stage, but the
crucial ways in which it isn't are not easy to specify.
– ERVING GOFFMAN

You need one. I don't care if you work in your basement. I don't care if you're an artist. A grown-up man needs at least one suit for special events. And once you have one, a good one which fits you and doesn't make you feel constricted and displayed like a prize cake, you will wonder why all your clothes aren't suits. You will want to buy three more. The standard men's uniform of loose but sober jacket and trousers is a remarkable confidence-giving garment: people will treat you differently when you are in a suit; they will look at you differently, they will ask your opinion, they will expect you to take care of trouble.

Women like men in suits. They may tell you otherwise – particularly if they are associated with a university in some way, or artists. Academics and students in, say, English, or philosophy, may squeal with disgust at the idea of a "dressed-up man"; artists will giggle, as if the idea is just embarrassing. This is because in these circles to admit attraction to a man in a suit is to betray the solidarity of one's working-class comrades and to delay the inevitable revolution. "Suit" is synonymous with "fascist baby-eater," or at the very least "insensitive boor" or "uptight suburbanite."

Obviously the honest expression of aesthetic response and/or sexual desire in these circles is not going to be exactly unfettered. In other words, don't believe a word of it.

I have found that there is almost no woman, no matter how many pairs of Birkenstocks she owns, no matter how devoted to her organic garden, who does not react with some slight tremor of the heart, some mild increase in blood pressure and dilation of the pupils, on seeing a man – particularly her own man – emerging from a cocoon of olive cotton and stepping forward in the sober costume of authority, his shoulders squared, his posture righted, with crisp collar and cuffs.

Part of the bad rap of suits, among bohemian men and women alike, is that our ostensible noncon-formists never seem to picture *good* suits. They always imagine bad ones: the ones their dad or their first husband wore to tense family events; they picture green double-breasted ones, or pale grey pinstripes with a waistcoat and slightly flared trousers, all of them hot and stiff and shiny and looking like faded posters for movies set in Atlantic City in the eighties.

I have often taken men, highly resistant men, shopping for their first grown-up suit. They have tended to be artistic types, writers usually, who have managed to make it well into their thirties without leaving their teenage uniform of jeans and running shoes, and who on occasion have never even learned to tie a tie. Each required a new suit for a special occasion (a wedding, an interview, a book tour), but I think each had also come to a stage in his career that made the suit symbolic of a decision to embrace a new kind of life, a life of success that would have a public component. In short, adulthood.

The procedure was for them fraught with misgivings both ideological and aesthetic. Several of them had old suits hanging in their closets, suits which they had been forced to buy by parents or bosses in previous lives (double-breasted and green) and which they felt they had to wear, like a kind of absurd, lit-up party hat, as one of the penances of certain excruciating obligatory events, such as weddings or graduations or Easter church services. They thought – consciously or not – that suits had to be rather tight and hot and itchy and that they had to be unfashionable and, bafflingly, that they had to be in pale colours. The first-time suit buyer nervously gravitates for some reason toward dove grey and beige. I suspect that this comes out of a fear of

"The first-time SUIT buyer nervously GRAVITATES for some reason toward DOVE GREY and BEIGE."

Fictional tailors

The gentleman's tailor, in the class-obsessed novels of the 1920s, is a stock figure. In the comic stories of P.G. Wodehouse, for example, dopey upper-class twits trust hatters and haberdashers as the ultimate authority on how they should look. Like small children, they simply let themselves be dressed.

Thus the tailor's relation to his client is of necessity an extremely intimate one. John le Carré, in *The Tailor of Panama*, has an expert tailor character who makes a standard joke with his clients about what side they chose to "dress": "Most of my gentlemen seem to favour the left these days. I don't *think* it's political."

The most famous gentleman's valet of the twentieth century, Wodehouse's Jeeves, has the task, among others, of dressing his master. Note that Jeeves is of a lower class than his master and yet is much more conservative. ☞

formality. My guys felt, instinctively, that a lighter-coloured suit was a kind of compromise, and that it was more youthful. Charcoal and navy, they thought, were "bankers' colours," colours that a young man doesn't feel he can carry off without being rich and grey-haired.

They could not have been more wrong, of course. If you are buying only one suit, that suit must be versatile, and a pale suit is only wearable in summer, which is not a long season in most of the G8 nations. You can, on the other hand, buy an extremely light-weight navy suit that is wearable year-round, and you can haul it out for cocktail parties and funerals alike. My friends tended to think that navy was somehow square – until they saw themselves in navy by Boss or Armani or Paul Smith or John Varvatos or the more forward lines of Canali or Zegna. All that defiant contrariness goes away when they come out of the change room wearing *both jacket and trousers* (this is important – you have to see the whole thing) of a soft, lightweight, dark-coloured new suit of elegant cut, with proper shoes, a white shirt, and a silver tie. They see this in the mirror and they are amazed. Their first expression is always one of surprise verging on shock; this quickly changes to a wide smile. They realize that a new part of themselves has been discovered. They look manly but not old; confident but not conservative.

If the new suit fits you properly, you will not feel "dressed up." It will not be constrictive or feel unnatural; it shouldn't make you feel self-conscious or delicate about how you stand or sit. You shouldn't notice it. And neither should other people: they should notice you, how strong and fit and clever you're looking.

Some Shopping Tips

This sounds obvious, but it needs saying: When you go shopping for suits, wear clothes that will match suits. Wear, or at least bring, the good shoes you will have on when you wear the suit. You would be amazed by how many guys undermine the shopping process by wearing their running shoes into the shop – there's no way you can tell what a suit is going to look like with the trousers all bunched up around your stained, scuffed, sorry-looking Nikes. (I think the unconscious motivation behind this act is to ensure that no suit will look good, so you don't have to make any decisions or spend any money.) Wear a white dress shirt, which matches any colour, and you can experiment with ties as well. And shave. Remember that salesmen can be snooty – they will judge a customer in superficial ways. They are going to expend more effort in helping you if it looks as if you want to play the game.

Quality

You can talk about the relative quality of fabrics and tailoring forever – and many people do – but first, a caveat. You will read a lot, if you read a lot of books

His role, like that of the Marxist tailor in Aldous Huxley's *Antic Hay*, is continually to tone his client down, to prevent him from wearing check waistcoats and garish spats, to keep him from embarrassing himself. Jeeves sternly confiscates his master's overly fashionable dinner jacket and gives it to the poor, and while Bertie may protest, he ultimately sighs and accepts Jeeves's nanny-like wisdom. This is real trust.

The tailor in *Antic Hay*, Mr. Bojanus, is probably the most complicated and amusing of these minor characters. Impeccably dressed and speaking in heavy cockney, he reprimands his upper-middle-class customer for looking "a trifle negleejay." Mr. Bojanus boasts that his clients are "the Best People," but is an admirer of Lenin and expects the day when the Best People will all be shot by the Red Guards. ⁊

Real Tailors

In contemporary North America, we tend to associate conservative taste with privilege. And being largely class-unconscious, we do not expect our tailors to have accents different from our own. Indeed, a successful clothier here means a successful businessman, which means the very pinnacle of social status. I can only dream of attaining the same level of prestige and influence enjoyed by the most successful retailers of this country.

The professional sartorial adviser is today more likely to encourage, rather than stifle, adventurousness in dress. And the job of the shopper is to resist the cajoling into tackiness of many a fast-talking salesman, who is, after all, our modern equivalent of the intimate tailor. Today, many men rely just as trustingly on a single salesman – "my guy at Fit-Rite" – who advises them on all purchases, from hankies to ties to ☞

like this one, about the perfection and desirability of a **bespoke** suit – that is, a suit handmade entirely to your measurements. I will discuss the advantages of such a luxury item. But it is important to remember that no suit will be forever in style. There is no point in going to Savile Row and spending six thousand dollars on a bespoke suit if it's going to look too short or too long or too wide in two years' time. Clothing is not an investment; it does not appreciate in value with age.

Similarly, I would say that even the best-quality off-the-rack suits – the Brionis and the Kitons and the Aquascutums and whatever – are not always the most stylish. Quality tends to be an older man's pursuit, and so it tends to be conservative. Fashionable ready-made suits – even very expensive ones by Dolce & Gabbana or Prada – are not necessarily well-made. In fact, they rarely are. Surprisingly, they are mass-produced, and have fused lapels and machine stitching and non-functional buttons. And who cares? If you want to look that hip, you are not going to be wearing such suits for ten years anyway.

But I am getting ahead of myself here, because we have not yet discussed what the signs of quality are.

Construction

If you have a great deal of money and have already bought enough original art for the walls of your house or apartment, you will want to consider having a suit made to measure. Note that there are subtle differences of vocabulary to describe degrees of labour here, and people do not always speak the same language in different establishments. Most men's shops will have a "made to measure" department which offers individually tailored suits. These suits are made from existing patterns, which are simply altered in size. There are only a few elements which can actually be altered: length, waist, chest, sleeves, and so on. You meet with a salesman to discuss the cut of suit you would like; he shows you a few styles, either from pictures or actual suits, and you choose one. Then you choose a fabric from a swatch book. You will be measured – chest, waist, shoulders, sleeves, inseam, and outseam – the suit will be put together, and then you come in for one fitting, to make final adjustments. The process can take anywhere from two days (in Hong Kong) to eight weeks (in large North American cities).

A truly custom-made suit, however – which is only available in large cities at a few expensive establishments – is made entirely from scratch. Beware both the word *bespoke* and the phrase *made to measure* – they may both mean, depending on the establishment, either made from patterns or custom-made. Make sure you know what you are getting and what you are paying for. In this book, I will use bespoke to mean fully custom-made.

Custom-made is, as you can imagine, rather expensive. The most famous place in the world for this process is a street in the City of Westminster, in

overcoats. This enables them to compress their yearly shopping into one forty-five-minute session, like having all their root canals done at once.

This is great if your guy is great. But how many men submit to the first fast talker who accosts them at the door? We can no longer trust our advisers to be the guardians of sobriety: I have been approached, in a highly respectable emporium, by a youth in a swanky collarless jacket and a hockey haircut who wanted me to try on a thousand-dollar Versace coat the colour of a fluorescent highway marker. Modern men can no longer fall helplessly and childishly into such a man's arms. We must take the responsibility to develop taste of our own.

Before you accept advice from a salesman, judge his own clothing. If he is wearing cowboy boots, tell him you are just browsing and wait for someone else.

London, called Savile Row, which houses a number of very famous tailors. (Why England is the origin of most conventions and most standards of quality in the world of masculine dress is an interesting question which we will get to in a moment.) So let us take this as our example of the *ne plus ultra* of the bespoke suit, and imagine that you have a few months to kill in London – since all these tailors are so popular there will be a waiting list, and the process takes at least six weeks and usually longer. So you have a few months to kill, and London is a fine place in which to kill them. You choose one of the imposing and archaic-looking establishments on Savile Row, you make an appointment, you come in for your first meeting with a tailor to discuss what kind of suit, what weight and style, and the tailor will design this suit only for you. A team of tailors is involved in the cutting: the head tailor (who is also the designer of the suit) is not actually called the tailor, but the cutter. The guys who work under him are called tailors, and they specialize in different parts of the suit – the jacket (called a coat on this street), the waistcoat, the trousers. (The jacket is called the suit-coat or suit-jacket in North America.)

Trained tailors are in very high demand the world over, for the art is dying out. It has always involved an apprenticeship of many years, long hours, hot, painstaking, and uncomfortable work, and relatively low pay. A large portion of the tailors in North America are of Italian background (in England they

> "Trained TAILORS are in very HIGH DEMAND the WORLD over, for the ART is DYING out."

tend to be Eastern European); they have learned their craft from their fathers or mothers and have grown up doing it. If they become successful, however, they end up owning their own shop and earning enough money to send their children to university – and then they lament that their sons, who gain degrees in accounting and law, have no interest in continuing the family tradition. I don't blame the offspring for wanting to leave the hot-iron steam and sweat of the tailor shop, but I feel for the men's shops that are constantly in desperate need of tailors for the made-to-measure boutiques, or even for everyday alterations.

The countries which are emerging to fill the gap in trained tailors are China, Vietnam, and Thailand – these are the new sources of skill for Western tailor shops, and we are grateful for it. These new talents will quite likely go through the same cycle of success, and a new search will begin.

But back to the process. This team of guys will take many more measurements than are normal for a pattern-based made-to-measure suit – there can be five different measurements of the legs and hips for the trousers alone. (This process demands pretty intimate contact, about which tailors are very professional and unembarrassed. They may even ask you on what side of the pant you like to "dress" – i.e., hang.) The measurements are both quantitative and qualitative. They will take into account all your body's irregularities: bow legs, belly, droops, arms

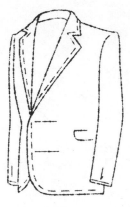

Tailor's basting

of uneven length, or shoulders of uneven height (which we all have to one degree or another).

The measurements then go to the cutter, who draws his patterns freehand on brown paper (imagine the confidence required). He cuts the fabric accordingly, and sends it to the team of tailors, who sew it together loosely with white thread, or "baste" it, so that you can try it on for the first fitting. Even if the team is working on your suit and no one else's, this process will take several days, because the total time required for the cutting and sewing is about forty hours. (This is how you know that the Hong Kong tailors who promise twenty-four-hour suits are using patterns and making minimal adjustments to them.)

So you come in for the first fitting several weeks later (because the tailor is not, as it turns out, working solely on your suit), and it is still very unfinished, with the front of the lapels not covered, and white basting everywhere. The cutter takes a look at you and decides what can be improved, marks the suit up again with chalk, takes the suit apart again, alters, and then begins the serious sewing. It is only at this stage that the coatmaker will begin to add the padding and stiffening agents that make a man's jacket: the canvas in the lapels, the padding in the shoulders. The lining will be sewn in. In good suits, the lining is of something called "Bemberg silk," which is actually rayon (Bemberg is a trade name). Lining is important even in superlightweight summer suits, if only around the shoulders, to ensure that the suit slides easily over your shoulders and does not catch on the buckles of your braces or whatever you are wearing.

You will come back for at least one and possibly even two more fittings. (Don't complain: Victorian men were known to suffer through up to twelve fittings of a new coat or suit.) The whole process will take months, but when you walk away with your perfectly fitting suit it will feel perfectly natural – it will not look new or fancy in any way. It will be as comfortable as pyjamas, but much less noticeable.

Note that the most expensive ready-made suits, such as those made by Brioni, are also handmade, and will often share the same indicators of labour-intensive quality. The most important signs of high quality, in suits made-to-measure or ready-made, are

Floating facings. The way the stiffening fabrics in the lapels (sometimes called interlinings, interfacings, or just facings) are introduced constitutes the most expensive difference between handmade and machine-made suits. In a very fine, handmade suit, the canvas inside the lapels is made of horsehair, which is light, strong, and elastic, and sewn onto the suit's fabric with silk thread, which is also very slightly elastic. The hundreds of tiny stitches used are quite loose. This lends the lapel "give" – if you take it between forefinger and thumb and roll it around you can feel it sliding slightly. This, in theory,

A good bespoke suit is as comfortable as pyjamas

gives the garment a more natural fit (although it is sometimes hard to perceive without touching it). You can also feel this "floating" interlining in heavy winter-weight suits at the bottom front of the jacket (the "skirt"). In mass-produced suits (which includes most designer labels), the interlinings are of some nasty mesh substance, and are fused with the outer wool of the suit, using glue and high heat.

Rolling lapels

Rolling lapels. A handmade jacket with a floating interlining will have lapels which "roll" away from the jacket – in other words, where the lapel folds into the jacket will not be a sharp crease, but a soft curve; the lapel rolls away from the jacket.

Matching patterns at the seams. The stripes or squares of the fabric will line up exactly at the shoulders or back seam, to create the illusion that the suit is not made up of stitched-together parts but all of a piece. You hang wallpaper on the same principle. It also shows that the cutter has carefully cut the parts of the suit from same bolt of cloth, paying attention to where they will come together.

Surgeon's cuffs

Surgeon's cuffs. If you have ever seen a dandy walking around with one button on his suit's sleeve undone, you may have wondered if he is simply being negligent. In fact, he is showing off: it is only in very expensive suits that the cuff buttons are functional. The idea is that you can roll up the sleeves to wash your hands (or operate on someone, which is where the name for this feature supposedly originated). In fact, it is only more evidence that the more labour involved in a thing's production, the more valuable it is, no matter how useless.

Fabric

It is astounding to think that the finest, silkiest fabrics in the world – the soft crepes and smooth flannels on elegant men in hotel lobbies in Monaco and Dubai – come from one of the world's plainest, messiest, and most rugged of animals. Most of it – especially the best of it – comes from huge herds of sheep in Australia and New Zealand and is milled into fabric in England and Italy.

Not one of the thousand attempts to introduce a textile for men's suitings that would supplant this most basic of natural fibres has succeeded. People make suits of cotton, sure, and linen and silk – and those have their place – but they are unusual suits for special situations. By far the vast majority of men's jackets and trousers are made of wool. No synthetic fibre can even come close to matching wool's comfort, fineness, affinity for dye, and elasticity.

It is really incredible stuff. It weaves into hundreds of different weights and blends and patterns. It has more longevity than most synthetics. It is warm even when it absorbs moisture; in fact, its capacity to absorb moisture gives it a cooling effect next to the skin in high heat. Its natural elasticity

"No SYNTHETIC fibre can even come CLOSE to matching wool's COMFORT, FINENESS, affinity for DYE, and ELASTICITY."

enables it to resist wrinkles. It's even flame-resistant. (It's true; just try lighting your suit on fire. It will smoke and singe a lot, but unless you soak it in gasoline, the flames will go out as soon as you remove the flame source.)

There are two basic kinds of wool yarn: **woollen** and **worsted**. To make both of them, you first "card" the loose wool, which means scraping it together into long strands.

To make woollen yarn you leave it at that: the resulting fibres will be coarser. You use this yarn for knitted textiles, which goes into such things as sweaters, and for suiting fabrics such as tweed, flannels, and meltons. (Melton is a napped or felt-like blazer fabric; the name is from a town called Melton Mowbray in Leicestershire, where hunting outfits were made.)

To make worsted yarn, which goes into woven fabrics, you have to twist the wool that has been carded and combed. The combing makes the fibres more parallel, with fewer ends exposed, so they are smoother. They are also chemically treated to remove their fuzzy edges. You can then twist the fibre very tightly to make very long, fine strands. Finely worsted wool is the basis of most suits.

If you have no time for history, you may skip this next bit, for it's not necessary knowledge, just interesting.

From the beginning of the Industrial Revolution, roughly at the end of the eighteenth century, the

British Isles dominated the world in the production of fine wool textiles. This is partly because it's colder there than in France or in Italy (where the greatest finery in Europe was made and worn), partly because there were a lot of sheep in Scotland, and partly because the British were more advanced in their industrialization than any other European country. This industrial dominance led to the rise of London, in the late eighteenth century, as the global tastemaker in men's clothing. English, and particularly London, cuts, styles, and tastes defined what a gentleman anywhere in the world would be wearing. This power really only began to wane in the late twentieth century, and is still vitally important. Which is why English values are a touchstone for so much of what is in this book.

Continental aristocrats first began wearing the styles of British country squires in the 1740s, and by 1760 the term "anglomania" was common in the French press. It wasn't just British fashion which was admired by the privileged French, either: British parliamentary democracy was attractive to a French society still labouring under the repressive despotism of an absolute monarchy. So British dress was symbolic of political freedom to the muzzled wealthy of the continent.

To illustrate this point, the fashion historian Farid Chenoune quotes a letter written by a British tourist after a visit to Paris in 1752. The suits he had made there, writes the casual Brit, "made

"London CUTS, STYLES, and TASTES defined what a GENTLEMAN anywhere in the WORLD would be WEARING."

complete Frenchmen of us. But for my part, Harry, I was so damned uneasy in a full-dressed Coat, with hellish long Skirts, which I had never been used to, that I thought myself as much deprived of my Liberty, as if I had been in the Bastile [*sic*]; and I frequently sighed for my little loose Frock [coat], which I look upon as an emblem of our happy Constitution; for it lays a Man under no easy Restraint, but leaves it in his Power to do as he please."

So politically important were gradations of dress in that era of upheaval that Balzac was later to write that 1789, the year of the French Revolution, was the year of the "debate between silk and broadcloth."

Central to British ideas of fashion – even in the middle of London – was the conception of the country house, rather than city palace, as the base of a gentleman's power. While French aristocrats of the eighteenth century were imprisoned in the gilded salons of Versailles, their British counterparts were out hunting and shooting on their estates. The French gentlemen wore knee-length coats over long waistcoats. This was impractical for riding; the English coats grew shorter, and so, eventually, did continental ones.

In other words, the modern-day suit, which so many consider to be impractical, evolved from what was basically a comfortable sporting outfit.

The dark colours we associate with the modern suit did not become prominent until toward the end of the eighteenth century, and even then only in

> "The MODERN-DAY suit EVOLVED from what was BASICALLY a comfortable SPORTING OUTFIT."

jackets – breeches were still usually cream or beige. And jackets and trousers were not made of the same fabric. Above one's knee breeches one wore a frock coat – a cutaway coat like a cross between a jacket and an overcoat. Trousers gradually replaced breeches in the first half of the nineteenth century, and the frock coat had to make up its mind as to whether it was a jacket or outerwear: eventually it was replaced by the overcoat, a looser coat which didn't hug the waist.

Because the overcoat didn't require as much tailoring, it heralded the end of the era in which every piece of clothing had to be custom-made; ready-made coats started to appear, and so began the rise to triumph of the ready-made.

Chenoune argues that the ascendancy of the ready-made, which dominated the coat market by the 1870s, led to another mass democratization of fashion and therefore of society itself. The effects of this were good and bad: traditional regional dress, for example, was to disappear from all over Europe. And European snobs joked that in America, because everyone could wear the same clothing, "gentlemen number in the millions."

The short jacket, the basis of the modern model, didn't appear in Europe until the 1860s, when tailors began sewing jackets and trousers of the same material for the first time. This was called the "lounge suit," a term still used in conservative British circles today.

It wasn't until well into the twenty-first century that Italian mills began to challenge British dominance in the manufacture of wool textiles. The great Italian textile revolution didn't really take off until the 1970s. Giorgio Armani's first men's collection was in 1975; the film *American Gigolo*, which dressed the handsome hustler Richard Gere entirely in Armani suits, appeared in 1980, and went a long way to defining that decade's image of elegance.

An interesting example of Italian textile dominance is seen in the factory of Ermenegildo Zegna, in the small northern Italian village of Trivero. Zegna took over his father's textile mill here in 1910; by 1938 he was exporting milled fabrics to over forty countries. In the 1960s the company launched its ready-to-wear line, which is now one of the most respected (if conservative) luxury brands in the world. Their strength was (and is) a combination of exquisite fabrics and traditional tailoring. They are probably best known for introducing an extremely fine wool fibre, which they called **Super 80s**. This high-twist wool enabled them to make suits that feel as light as silk. The number refers not to thread count but to the diameter of the fibres. Fine wools range from eighteen to twenty-four microns in diameter; an eighteen-micron fibre makes an "80s" grade fabric. Anything smaller than that is called "superfine." You will see the phrases *Super 100s* or *Super 120s* to describe even finer fabrics; these are commercial names, not technical ones, so they have no legal definitions. They just mean extremely fine wool, which will make featherlight and soft fabrics.

This development, and the rise of other great Italian designers, pretty much won pre-eminence for Italian textiles for suits, although British manufacturers will still argue the point. Suits have grown lighter over the past twenty years, so the luscious soft flannels that make British suits so comforting are not as popular, for they are heavier and really only useful in winter months. It is no longer necessary to have a rack of suits for each season: a dark suit in a Super 100s wool is appropriate for winter and not uncomfortable in spring or fall; it's only for the real dog days that you can allow yourself the indulgence of a pale grey or khaki suit, or something in silk or linen.

Today, the great Italian clothing manufacturers, including Armani, own their own textile mills, so they get first crack at buying up all the new fabrics. This means that even the best suit designers and manufacturers in the world don't have access to all the best wools.

You will hear the words *merino*, *cashmere*, and *angora* bandied about by unctuous salesmen: they are unctuous wools. **Merino** is a type of sheep, which provides the most expensive and softest wool for suits. **Cashmere** is an even finer animal hair, from goats whose origin is the Himalayan mountains. **Angora** comes from angora goats; the origin of the word is Ankara, in Turkey. Angora wool is what makes mohair (there is no such animal as a mo), which makes extremely fine and slightly lustrous fabric, perhaps best restricted to black formal wear. (Sometimes women's sweaters and mittens are made from a fluffy yarn also called angora wool, which is actually a blend of sheep's wool and angora *rabbit* fur. This is only to confuse you; there is no rabbit fur in men's suits.)

It is difficult to dye any of these yarns once they are woven, so most yarns of whatever origin are dyed before they are spun (giving rise to the term "dyed-in-the-wool"). Mixed colour and pattern in the final fabric must therefore be created by inter-weaving threads of differing colours.

There are a few standard patterns with standard names. Here are most of them:

Houndstooth

Hopsack is a coarse, loose weave.

Crepe is a very light fabric made from very fine, high-twist wool; it has a slight sheen to it and is faintly rough to the touch.

Flannel is a catch-all term for any fabric with a smooth, napped surface.

Twill is a kind of weave that makes a diagonal line.

Gabardine is made with a tight twill weave and tends to be of a solid colour.

Houndstooth, another variation of the twill weave, is a pattern found in both tweeds and worsteds, made of jagged, broken checks.

Herringbone

Herringbone is also a twill weave, but made by

alternating the pattern of the diagonal line to make a V pattern.

Glen plaid – short for Glen Urquhart, a Scottish clan – is a pattern of small checks alternating with larger squares, usually in light grey. Also called **Prince of Wales plaid** (or *Prince de Galles* on the continent), particularly if there are squares or fine lines of one more colour overlaid – not, as one might assume, after the famous dandy who became Edward VIII and later the Duke of Windsor, but after his grandfather, Edward VII, who wore this pattern in sporting suits when he was Prince of Wales.

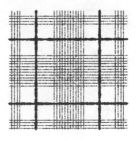

Glen plaid

Gun-club check is similar, using three colours to form a larger check over a smaller check.

Windowpane check is a more austere pattern of large, plain, open squares in fine lines.

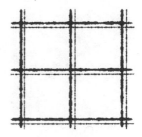

Windowpane check

The smallest checks are called **bird's eye** or **nailhead**: tiny dots, or tiny diamonds with a dot in the centre, usually so small as to look solid from a distance. **Sharkskin** – wool fabric with a slight shine – is made from weaving two colours across each other so as to catch the light in different ways as they move.

Nailhead check

A coarse tweed, or raw silk, may have an irregular fuzziness, caused by knots on the surface; these are poetically known as **slubs**.

The louder patterns – large houndstooth, for example, or coloured **tartan** – are still best kept to tweed suits, for country or casual Friday wear;

Pinstripe

Chalkstripe

the finer the wool, the more subtle your pattern should be.

Pinstripe is a fine stripe of a lighter colour, regularly spaced.

Chalkstripe is the same thing but not as sharply defined – it's a line that's faintly blurred or indistinct, about the width of a line made by a tailor's chalk.

Salesmen will often praise a fabric's **"hand."** What they mean is the feel of it to the touch.

The finest wool is made by only a few mills and used by almost every designer. The Italian firm Loro Piana, for example, is generally regarded as a summit of luxury, as is the French mill Dormeuil. Canali, Zileri, and Brioni all use Loro Piana wools.

Although the new wools are extremely light, many mills are mixing them with small proportions of other more summery fabrics – linen, silk, mohair, rayon, or viscose – for a faint sheen or a nubbly finish. As long as the wool makes up at least 60 per cent, the suit is formal.

Cut

The most important aspect of a suit is not how it is made but how it looks. The silhouette is what people will see from afar, and so the cut is a consideration more primary than the fabric or the construction.

There are two basic designs for men's suits: single-breasted, which is the more common, and double-breasted, which means that the jacket overlaps in the front. Let's start with the basic single-breasted, which is the foundation of a man's city attire.

From the 1970s to the 1990s, most single-breasted business suits had only two buttons, and you fastened only one of them (the top one). As the **button stance** was quite low – that is, the top button was positioned below the chest – the suit left quite an expanse of shirt and tie visible.

Some salesmen will refer to the place where the lapels meet (usually, where the top button is) as the **gorge** – which is not, strictly speaking, accurate. The gorge is actually the seam where the collar meets the lapel – in other words, it's where the notch is. But gorge and button stance are closely related: the higher the button stance, the higher the gorge. This is changing: as of this writing, the gorge is rising and the button stance is dropping. Your own body type will determine which placement is right for you. If you are short, you should consider a high gorge: the longer lapel will add to an impression of verticality.

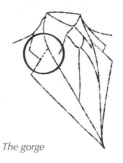

The gorge

The three-button suits which returned to fashion in the 1990s were not quite the same as their predecessors of the 1950s: the jackets were slightly longer, the gorge higher, the silhouette narrower, the armholes smaller and higher. This basic style has remained in fashion, with a few variations.

Four-button suits were briefly popular at the end of the twentieth century but quickly disappeared again. And now there is a return to a two-button design – but again, it is just different enough from the old style that you cannot simply raid your closet for your old 1980s suits and wear them again. (Fashion designers would never let you do that; it would make them redundant.) The new two-buttons have a nipped waist. This hourglass shape is often what salesmen mean when they say that a look is "tailored"; it makes them look nostalgic – like hip suits of the mid-1960s, just before lapels were to grow insanely wide.

A new development to accompany this return to the two-button silhouette is the peaked rather than notch lapels with single-breasted suits.

Peak lapels usually go on double-breasted suits, or on single-breasted dinner jackets (tuxedos). They look dressier, more formal. The pairing of peak lapels with single-breasted closures is a very forward trend, but it seems set to last.

Lapel width varies from decade to decade. We are in a narrow-to-medium phase right now. You should coordinate, very roughly, the width of your tie with the width of your lapels; that is, a very wide tie will look awkward with very narrow lapels, and vice versa. Wide lapels will also look wrong with very tiny shirt collars.

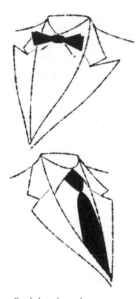

Peak lapels and notch lapels

Single-Breasted Suits

Let's start with the classic: the single-breasted, three-button suit. A very dressy, conservative suit of this type will have two **vents** (slits) in the sides, toward the back. The vent originated, again, in England, to facilitate sitting astride a horse. Now it makes the suit hang more naturally, particularly if you want to stick your hands in your pockets (which you won't be doing too often), or straddle a motorcycle (which you may do as often as you like). A suit with two vents – often called **side vents** – is the most formal- (and English-) looking; a suit with no vents is the most casual. I would go either with two or none: the single-vented jacket is conservative, but I see it as a spineless compromise, and it tends to part in an awkward manner, displaying your trouser seat whenever you put your hands in your pockets.

Giorgio Armani revolutionized modern suit design by resolutely producing ventless suits throughout the 1980s and 90s; his very recognizable silhouette – soft shoulders, long and drapey jacket – has been copied by many American designers. Depending on your build, it can look stunning or rumpled, at worst kind of *Miami Vice* flashy.

Personally, I like vents. But they are best on a skinny person. A ventless jacket can be flattering to a pronounced backside: a wide bum, in the absence of a good alterationist, can exaggerate the vent and make the jacket flare around the hips. So this choice is up to you.

You will hear talk of the "American-style" suit in conservative menswear establishments. This is a rather dated term now, but it needs explaining if only for historical interest. The American company

How many buttons to button?

It's distressing how many men you see wrapped in their new suits like sausages, all three buttons bursting. These are men who may be earning into the top tax bracket – and their suits are not cheap – and they still look like uncomfortable school-boys. Let's get this straight: on any single-breasted suit jacket, no matter how many buttons it bears, you never do up the bottom one.

That much is agreed by all, but opinions differ on which of the remaining two buttons you do fasten. Older men, who wore three-button suits in the 1950s and 60s, still swear that the only acceptable button to close is the middle one. However, most salesmen today, creatures of trend that they are, will do up the top two for you. That's the current practice. And those who want to look youthful and daring, ☞

what we like to call the Advanced Class, will do up only the top button, for a flared-silhouette, I-know-Milan kind of look.

One disadvantage of the old-fashioned middle-button-only practice is that if you are wearing a heavy wallet in your inside pocket its weight will pull one lapel downward and throw the whole line out. If you close the top two buttons, it will support the wallet and prevent the front of the suit from "cracking."

When wearing a four-button jacket, in theory, you do up the three top buttons only, but that is useless information for you, because you have already piled up your old four-buttons and given them to the poor, haven't you? ॐ

Brooks Brothers – the arbiters of all things preppy – introduced a style of suit in the 1950s which was markedly different in cut from the English suits then being worn by East Coast establishment figures. The Brooks Brothers "Sack Suit," also known as the Ivy League look, was boxy, not fitted – straight up and down, not tailored at the waist. The shoulders were softer and narrower, not as stiffly padded as those in upright English models. The jacket was relatively short, particularly by today's standards, and had one centre vent. This comfortable if unsexy suit became the uniform of the American businessman, and it definitely influenced Italian designers, who also produce loose and less stiffly constructed suits.

However, there are so many variations in suit design these days, across all national borders, that it is hard to identify one particular national style.

Brooks Brothers probably still makes these square 1950s-style suits. I wouldn't know – ask your dad.

Double-Breasted Suits

These always seem dressier to me, and flashier, than other suits. They are often favoured by portly men, as their uniformly cylindrical silhouette camouflages the bulbous figure. But I think they look slick on slender men, too, particularly if they are fairly fitted.

Here's the tricky thing to note about double-breasted suits: the number of buttons varies. Again, the more modern the suit, the higher the buttons will go, and the less shirt-and-tie will be exposed. There are two rows of buttons, and only some of them are functional. When salesmen say "four on two," they mean that there are four buttons on the front of the jacket, but only the bottom two are below the fold of the lapel. The top two will not be functional, nor will they be lined up vertically with the bottom two. This will be a very out-of-date, 1980s-looking suit. (Think *American Psycho*.) "Six on four" is the more common model today: it means that there are six buttons on the front of the jacket, with four of them below the end of the lapel. This produces a higher gorge, and a narrower silhouette. This is the design favoured by the Prince of Wales, and he looks damn good in it. The trick of it is to have quite a high button stance – that is, the suit will look quite stern and tubular, not droopy and relaxed.

"four on two" double-breasted suit

Note that on the Prince's suits, the lapel rolls up on the chest, not below the waistline, as with old-fashioned six-on-two configurations.

If you want to look really natty, try a six-on-six double-breasted. (You had better be tall.) All six buttons are (or appear to be) closed. This look was popular until the 1930s. It looks a little fussy and military today, but also nostalgic in a way that can be dramatically stylish.

"six on four"

Double-breasted suits nowadays always have peak lapels, double vents, and fairly pronounced shoulders. They look particularly good with spread shirt collars.

"six on six"

All the functional buttons on a double-breasted jacket should be kept fastened at all times – and that means including the inside "**shank**" button, which must be done up before the outside button is closed. There is nothing less dignified than a man wandering about with the skirts of his jacket flapping around like albatross wings (Mr. David Letterman, take note). The front flaps of the double-breasted jacket are just too heavy not to sag when they are undone; this will throw off the jacket's entire line.

Fit

The jacket should completely cover your bum. The bottom of the jacket will line up with the beginning of your thumb – the knuckle – when your hands are at your sides. Another way of judging the correct length is to see that the jacket is exactly half as long as the distance from your collar's seam to the floor. But these guidelines vary depending on a man's build; a short man, for example, will want to avoid long jackets. A good salesman or tailor will be able to tell you if the jacket is the correct length.

Sleeve length is also a personal issue. I always find that tailors try to pin my sleeves too long. They argue that the sleeve will shorten as I raise my hands above my head. What do they think I'm going to be doing in my suit, playing basketball? It is crucial to me that a half-inch of shirt cuff be visible at all times at my wrist, and so I sternly demand that tailors work against their instincts on this one. I note with some satisfaction that most men around me seem to wear their jacket sleeves slightly too long.

The most important part of a suit, in terms of fit, is the shoulders: in the class-conscious world of powerful men, nothing says neophyte louder than a gape at the collar or a roll in the shoulder. The shoulders must fit *perfectly*, and that's that. Here's how: (1) There will be no bump or wrinkle in the fabric across the back beneath the collar; (2) The collar of the jacket must be flat against the shirt collar all the time. If the shoulders don't fit properly, there will occur a gap which the historian and essayist Paul Fussell calls the "prole gape" (as in proletarian). Now, most off-the-rack suits will present you with these flaws as soon as you try them on, but don't panic: an experienced tailor can make a few nips and tucks and correct these easily.

The other thing to avoid is a tight fit around the middle. You don't want the suit to be ballooning out around you, but neither do you want any disfiguring pull on the centre button. If there are wrinkles on the front of the jacket when you close it – the tell-tale X of tension lines – then the jacket is too small.

Shoulders

Yes, suits are designed to flatter the male figure by exaggerating the shoulders: the shoulders are secondary sexual characteristics. They have been the focal point of military uniforms – on which fluttering epaulettes serve to enhance them even further

When to undo?

The buttons are there for a reason. The suit is meant to be seen with the jacket closed: it makes the lines perfect. So unbutton only when you sit down, and keep your jacket done up whenever you are standing. Besides, the loose, flapping jacket looks a little slobby: we don't want to see your belt and whatever hangs over it. ⁂

– for centuries. Suits make drooping shoulders square, and effect the overall tubular outline that men prefer to their real shapes. Yes, we all want our shoulders to be wider than our hips, but be careful: it is easy to go overboard with shoulder pads. Big, blocky square shoulders are no longer in fashion. (And besides, they make short men look wide.) Keep the shoulders soft and as natural as possible, even sloping a little. Avoid padding.

Trousers

The principal variations are these:

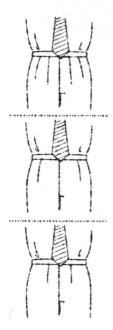

[from top]
Double pleats
Single pleats
Single "reverse" pleats

Pleats. Conventional wisdom has it that pleats at the waist are flattering to the man with a swelling middle. This may be true, but the sad fact for paunchy men is that a bat's-wing fan of pleats is increasingly out of fashion. If you only feel comfortable in pleated trousers, at least stick to a single pleat. Note that pleats may be folded outward or inward. A single "reverse" pleat – that is, a pleat folded inward – is another sober modern alternative, for it produces a flatter trouser front. Men who are in good trim will enjoy the opportunity to wear the coolest option of all: the classic flat-front trouser. If you can, do it; it is a privilege.

Fullness in the thigh. Pleated trousers tend to be fuller in the thigh and taper slightly to the ankle. Contemporary suits, however, are rather

narrow in silhouette (with some exceptions, notably
Armani), so you may want to avoid very baggy
trousers from now on.

Width at the ankle. Obviously, the wider
the thigh, the more it will taper as it approaches the
shoe. But full trousers will still be wider at the ankle
than narrow ones. Personally, I like the fifties look
of narrow trousers, all the way down. Now this
leads to the delicate discussion of . . .

Trouser Break

The **break** is the beginning of a fold in the bottom
of your trouser leg as it brushes your shoe. If the
trousers are too long, the fold will be too pronounced – like a sheet bagging around your ankle.
If the trousers are too short, there will be no break
at all. The art of hemming trousers is a fine one,
and you can't always trust the tailor who trundles
out of his backroom to hastily pin you up and rush
away again. You have to keep your eye on him. Make
sure the waist of the pants is cinched exactly as
loosely as you will wear it, and sitting exactly where
it will sit when you are relaxed and not standing
stiffly at attention. Insist that the tailor pin up *both*
trouser legs – many people have legs of slightly
uneven length. Ensure that the back of the pant (at
the heel) is about two and a half centimetres off the
floor, and that there is one break – not a full fold,
just a break.

*You want just one break in
the trouser leg (below), and
with narrow-cut pants (top)
no break at all*

A very narrow, stovepipe trouser leg demands a different approach. If you hem those to your usual length, measuring about two and a half centimetres from the floor and allowing for a break in front, they will bag up around your ankles and make you look childish. Stovepipes should be a good three to four centimetres shorter than wider legs, with no break in front – just kissing the top of the shoe. It's a sleek, taut look, not a drapey one. If you're worried about the rear edge sticking out, have the hem cut on an angle, slightly longer in the back.

"The GREAT champion of TROUSER CUFFS was Edward VII."

Cuffs or No Cuffs

Called "turn-ups" in Britain, they became popular in the nineteenth century, again through the influence of outdoor sports: the fashion arose simply out of rolling up one's trouser legs in muddy terrain. According to Farid Chenoune, members of the Windsor Cricket Club were seen rolling up the bottoms of their trousers as early as 1860; this undoubtedly influenced non-members eager to be seen as equally sporting and privileged. But the great champion of trouser cuffs was, as with many such innovations, Queen Victoria's son, Edward VII. When he was Prince of Wales, he was seen at the races at Ascot – one of the dressiest days in the English social calendar – with his trousers rolled up. It was a rainy day, and he had been walking around some paddocks, inspecting the horses; it was a practical gesture, and yet the social impact was enormous. "Permanent turn-ups" came into fashion in the 1890s. The trend caused consternation in Parliament when Viscount Lewisham appeared in the House of Lords wearing turn-ups – a shockingly casual state of dress.

Savile Row tailors still use the abbreviation PTU for cuffs.

Cuffs are no longer shocking, but their desirability is often a topic of heated discussion. There are those who insist that all trousers should be cuffed, and those who insist that a certain type of modish suit should never be cuffed at all. The advantage of a trouser cuff is that it gives weight to the bottom of the trouser to prevent it from getting hiked up by your socks or flapping about. Some clever tailors will even sew a fabric tape around the inside bottom of your trousers, to add extra weight. Be aware that plain bottoms can be finished by machine in about three minutes, whereas cuffs require some hand basting and take much longer, so a cuffed trouser is indicative of care and attention.

Cuffs are certainly always desirable on trousers with wide or full legs. It is only with very hip, narrow trousers that they might be questioned. There are no rules here, however; you may rely on your own personal taste. Generally, cuffs have now come to be regarded as formal; casual suits don't need them, nor do trousers meant for wearing with sports jackets.

Trouser cuffs vary in width, from about three to four centimetres. The width tends to correspond to

"CUFFS have now come to be regarded as FORMAL."

the width of the jacket's lapels: narrow lapels mean minimal cuffs, and vice versa. Short men will want to avoid very wide cuffs, as they shorten the leg.

Personally, I think that cuffed trousers are desirable on any dressy suit's trousers, as they give the trouser a finished look. They are always inappropriate, however, with very formal wear, such as black tie or morning suits.

Suspenders

The oak back, or V-back, houses buttons to anchor your suspenders

The British call them braces, so snooty menswear providers use the term as well. There are huge advantages to wearing suspenders, chief among them being comfort. No tight belt! No tight waistband! And you can adjust the height of the waistband, and the exact degree of break on your shoes. It is five minutes' work for a tailor to add a **suspender set** – the buttons inside the waistband – to your suit trousers (he'll still charge you twenty dollars for it, but it's worth it).

Real dandies who can afford to have bespoke suits made sometimes ask for a rise at the back of the trousers that houses two buttons, facing inward, a sort of flap which covers the small of your back. This is called an **oak back** or **V-back**. It is a 1920s look which can look either quaint or trying-too-hard. It looks a little undressed if you take your jacket off. But you won't be taking your jacket off anyway, will you?

Now don't take my recommendation for suspenders as encouragement to go all Wall Street tacky with them. Braces should be sober – dark and invisible. I don't want to see them. The frat-boy love of displaying wide, bright, goofily patterned suspenders is immature: it's like parading around giggling about your happy-face boxer shorts. We don't care.

I needn't tell you, if you have got this far, that braces must have actual buttonholes in them; clip-on braces are completely unacceptable for adults. Also avoid the stretchy elastic kind: buy plain cotton webbing, with leather tabs for buttons.

And you must choose between suspenders and a belt; do not wear both.

Waistcoats

I find it rather a shame that waistcoats – called vests in America – have almost completely disappeared from modern suits; I find them rather distinguished. Part of the reason for their disappearance is that across Europe – even in Britain – buildings tend to be well-heated these days, and the suit is no longer required to provide as much insulation. Suits generally are lighter than they have ever been. But waistcoats are still to be found – either in very conservative or very forward designs. If you like the slightly fussy look that they impart, then by all means indulge (noting that the addition of a waistcoat will raise the price of your suit). If you do, pay attention to the following details:

- In Britain, tailors pronounce it "weskit"; so do old-school establishments across the pond.

- Never do up the bottom button of a single-breasted waistcoat.
- The waistcoat should fit smoothly around the trunk, with no wrinkles or sagging. But if it's too tight, you will face the unfortunate sausage comparison once again. It's a tricky business.
- The top of the waistcoat will be visible between the jacket's lapels when the jacket is closed. The back of the waistcoat will be longer than the front. The two points at the bottom front should just cover the waistband of the trousers.
- If nostalgic affectation is your game, here is the place to indulge it. Attach your pocket watch's fob – the leather tab at the end of the chain – to a waistcoat button, then drop the watch in the waistcoat pocket. You might want to get some cigars, and maybe a monocle, to complete your costume.
- Waistcoats for regular business suits should be single-breasted and have no lapels. Some double-breasted suits from 1900 to 1940 were made with double-breasted waistcoats with small lapels; this looks very tight and fussy now. The only outfit which might justify a double-breasted waistcoat is a morning suit, which we will visit in another chapter.

"NEVER do up the bottom BUTTON of a single-breasted WAISTCOAT."

Other Details

The finishing around a suit's pockets will also tell you something about its quality. A great deal of sewing goes into pockets – and the more there is, the pricier the garment. The pocket is inserted into the lining; the double line of stitching above or below the opening creates a very narrow band called a **welt**. If a pocket has a welt it is called a **besom** pocket (also called a **jetted** pocket); if it has two it is called a **double besom**. A besom pocket may or may not have a flap over the opening. If your suit jacket has flaps over the pockets, wear the flaps out, as they are meant to be worn, rather than tucking them into the pocket.

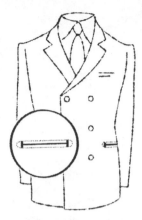

The besom pocket, with D-tacks

If your suit is really high quality, the ends of the besom will be finished with a **D-tack** – a little semicircle of stitching that joins top and bottom besom.

Patch pockets are sewn onto the outside of the jacket and indicate a more casual suit or blazer.

Some English suits with an hourglass silhouette will have an extra flap pocket, usually on the right-hand side, directly above the right hip pocket. This is called a **ticket pocket**, from the uniforms of British train conductors. If it is slightly slanted, it is more likely to be called a **hacking pocket**. The word comes from "hacking jacket," a practical outdoor jacket for riding ("hacking" is riding at a leisurely pace along a road – it comes from "hackney," which meant a horse of average quality).

The flap pocket, with ticket pocket above it, and the more casual patch pocket

Again, the hacking pocket can look distinguished or overly fussy, depending on the suit.

Some made-to-measure establishments are adding a large inside pocket to the bottom of the jacket, for

Beware the dry cleaner

Dry cleaning is a harsh chemical process and will reduce the life expectancy of your suit. Do it frequently and your delicate wool suit will first grow shiny and then start to disintegrate. It should be reserved for the severest of stains. Most stains will come out with a damp cloth, or simply by brushing with a stiff lint-brush. If you've spent a sweaty night in a smoky bar, the odour will come out if you hang the suit up in an open window overnight. (Don't try this in a ground-floor window, or your suit might be gone by morning.) If the suit is really wrinkled, say, after travelling in a suitcase, hang it up in the bathroom while you're taking a shower. The steam will relax the fabric and the wrinkles will come out. Wool has a sort of memory: it will revert to its usual shape if you hang it up in a closet for a ☞

a cellphone. I seriously disapprove of this measure, as even the smallest cellphone is heavy enough to throw the line of your suit out and make a bulge. Try to minimize what you put in your pockets – phones, PDAs, datebooks, and massive key chains are what briefcases are for. A single slim wallet, kept in an inner breast pocket (not the trouser back pocket, where it will push the back of your jacket out), a pen in the other breast pocket, a house key and a car key on a single ring, and a plain white handkerchief, kept in a trouser pocket, are the maximum freight a fine suit can bear.

How Many Do I Need?

Well, need is one thing, desire is another. You need as many suits as you can afford. If you work in a business that requires a suit every day, then you will need a closetful, eventually – but on your first day on the job, need only one. Make this one plain and flexible: a single-breasted three-button in charcoal – dark grey, almost black but not quite.

Why charcoal? Why not black? Black is a nighttime colour; on a sunny day it tends to look either ecclesiastical or mobsterish. It is also harder to match with shirts and ties – the contrast is too great. Charcoal goes with almost any colour.

You will buy this suit in a very fine wool – Super 100s or above – so that it is lightweight and you can wear it on warm spring or fall days, or even in the summer. But keep it dark.

After receiving your first paycheque you can buy one more suit: plain navy. Also single-breasted. No whimsical linens or plaids yet: you must build the basics first. Navy is equally sober, looks sharp on anybody, and is also a great match for most colours – particularly pinks, purples, and reds.

Next paycheque, next suit. This is one you can have a little fun with, be a little more expressive: a charcoal with a pinstripe, say, if you live in a northern climate. (You may, if you live in a place where it is hot most of the time, skip this step and go directly to a lighter grey – a mid-grey, not a dove grey.) The pinstripe suit is fun: it can look very fashionable or very conservative, depending on how you dress it up. In any case, it's a little flashier. You can also consider a double-breasted suit at this point.

Now you have your three winter suits, you can consider a lighter weight, slightly lighter colour for summer.

Before we go on, I must make a digression. Every man fantasizes optimistically, in the first few weeks of hazy weather, about a cool, dandyish tropical suit. We see them – white, cream, pink, pistachio – in movies about Miami and L.A., in magazine spreads (shot in Miami and L.A.) set poolside and on rooftop gardens. We see the Great Gatsby on the rolling lawns of his estate, in Panama hat and white bucks; we see Ricardo Montalban in white linen welcoming guests to Fantasy Island. The magazines show us tall, dark men in sandals wearing crisp

while. You can also press a suit yourself, with an iron, if you need your trouser crease a little sharper. Make sure the iron is not too hot, or the wool will develop a shine. For particularly delicate fabrics, put a damp cloth between the iron and the trousers. ❧

baby-blue suits, talking on cellphones in Cal-Ital adobe restaurants.

These images are like ads in the travel section: they make you think everything is better somewhere else. And when you're sweating in traffic you think, hey, it's just as hot here as it is in L.A., in fact bloody Abu Dhabi couldn't possibly be hotter than this cab at this moment. A white suit wouldn't be inappropriate here. Hey, I could do that, couldn't I?

Well, you can't. A white, cream, or pastel suit anywhere north of Alabama is foppish. Picture not the Great Gatsby but Tom Wolfe, who fancies himself an iconoclast in his white three-piecer. Note how his haircut is really a little, well, mullettish, and how the suit's nattiness now reminds you not of the elegant 1930s but of the disco 1970s. Who wants to look like Colonel Sanders?

The white suit is a symbol of the man who won't fit in, of outsiderness. In the 1951 British film *The Man in the White Suit*, Alec Guinness is a socially inept scientist who invents an indestructible fabric, to the horror of textile workers and their factory-owning bosses. The mild-mannered Guinness makes and wears a suit of it – double-breasted, no less – something a Colombian planter would wear. In the grey industrial landscape, the suit's blazing whiteness is in itself hilarious, a garish beacon of everything that is not English about this product.

Interestingly, up to about the time of that film,

"A white, cream, or PASTEL suit anywhere north of ALABAMA is FOPPISH."

America was a land of dandies when it came to summer suits. In Theodore Dreiser's 1900 novel *Sister Carrie* (a book which obsesses at length over sartorial detail), male characters wear tight suits with low-cut waistcoats, pink-and-white striped shirts, tan shoes, and grey fedoras. As late as the thirties, a northeastern establishment man could wear a striped seersucker with bow tie and straw boater and not be thought of as eccentric.

The change came with the beginning of the Cold War, when the armies of returning GIs exchanged olive drab for grey flannel. By 1964, Saul Bellow could render his character Herzog ridiculous merely by dressing him in a candy-striped summer jacket: "Dressed in Italian pants, furled at the bottom, and a blazer with slender lapels, red and white, he avoided full exposure in the triple, lighted mirror." Taxi drivers comment sardonically on Herzog's jacket for the rest of the book.

Now only the manliest of ancient Washingtonians can carry off an entire suit made of seersucker (the puckered, striped cotton fabric) without the average television viewer doubting their sexual orientation. (Seersucker goes all acid-trippy on television, anyway.) And bow ties have become proudly nerdy badges of right-wing-newspaper affiliation.

Italians, in Italy, can get away with pastels in cotton and linen, but it's hotter for longer there. And even in Italy, the man who owns a peach-coloured suit already owns five or ten more practical suits. Here, with casual Fridays still persisting in many places, a man needs even fewer.

Note that I do not lump khaki, tan, or beige in with the dandies. In fact, the khaki cotton suit (very fine cotton only; it can be as soft as silk) is as preppy an outfit as exists, especially when paired with a blue shirt and striped tie. I'm bored by that look, but I do like those suits because they can be dressed down – with a polo shirt and no socks – for casual evenings and weekends.

But any light-coloured suit is a luxury for a man with a limited budget. My next sober step, for summer, would be that mid-grey, lightweight suit. Either plain grey or glen plaid – in wool.

So, we are up to four suits. You are pretty much okay for the office, but you could always do with a going-out suit, for cocktail parties and clubs. This is where plain black comes in. A black suit is versatile in that it can go up or down: with a blue shirt and tie it looks respectable (if a little dull); pair it with a flowing rayon sports shirt, untucked, and a pair of pointy Chelsea boots and you're on your way to a music-video awards ceremony. Pair it with slip-on shoes and a black T-shirt and you're on your way to brunch and shopping. The black suit is, in the evening at least, invisible and always stylish.

Once you have five practical suits, your next suit purchase can be a little more whimsical or indulgent. Now – and only now – can you consider a

"The BLACK suit is, in the EVENING at least, INVISIBLE and always STYLISH."

tweed suit (a great luxury, as almost entirely useless except for casual Fridays) or a linen suit, or some combination of wool and silk, or even brushed cotton, for summer. Or something brown. And now is the time to consider fashion-forward suits with unusual detailing – a suit with patch pockets, for example, or a black suit with white stitching, or a black suit with a touch of polyester in it, for a little shine, or a high-buttoning six-on-six double-breasted suit. Consider a casual-but-flashy suit, for non-business but flirtatious events, such as receptions and Christmas parties: something by Versace or Prada or Paul Smith or the "Hugo" line of Hugo Boss, or the "Vestimenta" line of Armani, or the "Z" line of Zegna, or, hell, why not, Alexander McQueen. (I am assuming you have been promoted by this time.) At this point, you can start to begin buying suits not because you need them but because you like them.

So, to sum up, here are your essential suits in order of purchasing priority:

1) charcoal
2) navy
3) pinstripe
4) lighter grey (summer-weight)
5) black (fashion-forward or casual, for evenings)
6–100) anything you like

And you will need a couple of sports jackets and blazers, which we can now proceed to discuss.

CHAPTER THREE

JACKETS

Fashion, n. A despot whom the wise ridicule and obey.
– AMBROSE BIERCE

I have often wondered how garments so obviously impractical to wear during heavy exertion – such as silk shirts or navy blazers – acquired the label "sport." Why is a wool three-button jacket called a sports jacket? (In Britain, at least: in America one says sport jacket or sport coat, without the "s.") This is just one of the strange idiosyncrasies of the sartorial industry, and like most such idiosyncrasies it has its origin in British history. Tweed or hopsack jackets that were "odd" – that is, not part of a suit – were not meant for wear while actually rowing or playing polo, but for wear while *watching* these sports. They were sideline attire, or gin-in-the-clubhouse attire.

Now that baseball caps and T-shirts are deemed appropriate for sport-watching, fine buttoned jackets seem neither casual nor dressed-up; they are for artistic, academic, or otherwise creative milieux, a compromise between the severity of a suit and the frumpiness of a sweater.

It's true that younger men tend to be squeamish about sports jackets. They're so often tweed, for one thing, which has professorial overtones. And they do look a little square. Almost as square as blazers do – and let's face it, blue blazers with brass buttons, particularly when worn with grey flannel trousers and a striped tie, pretty well all come attached to a doctor's pager and a Jaguar; you are unlikely to see your favourite athlete or pianist gracing the boulevards in one.

But before weighing the merits of these garments, let's attack the terminology.

The difference between a sports jacket and a blazer is chiefly in the material: where a sports jacket is textured and sometimes patterned, a blazer is of a solid, dark colour (usually navy, although black, bottle green, and bright colours are also seen in the United States) and of a smooth worsted or napped fabric. It is said that the name originated with the HMS *Blazer*, whose captain designed the prototype jacket for his sailors on the occasion of an inspection by Queen Victoria in 1837. This explains why the jacket is still usually seen adorned with naval-style brass or fake brass buttons. In the early twentieth century it became the uniform of sports teams, particularly cricket teams, who wore blazers with loud stripes in their institutional colours. It is still properly worn only to sporting events. The blazer is not a formal outfit and should not be worn with grey flannels to a funeral or a meeting of the Board of Directors; these require a suit.

Meanwhile, the traditional blazer, in a light worsted or hopsack wool, with brass buttons, either single-breasted or double, has become a symbol of the older man. It's simply not fashionable any more. Which isn't to say it doesn't still carry a certain goofy charm, as would a handlebar moustache or a pipe. It's a mark of the establishment, but it also imparts a hint of the aging playboy: one expects navy-blazer-wearers to sport ascots and driving gloves. (It's really just the buttons I object to. Remove those loud brass buttons, replace them with black horn, and you have a useful jacket, in black or navy – particularly in soft wool and cashmere with a napped texture.)

The sports jacket derives from civilian outdoor wear. Its ancestor is the Norfolk jacket, named after the Duke of Norfolk, which was worn in the nineteenth and early twentieth centuries for shooting and riding. The Norfolk jacket was of sturdy tweed and had a built-in half-belt (technically called a "self-fabric" belt) at the back. Tweed jackets, made of heavy wool, were worn as rugged country wear for the first half of the century and were not worn in the city. Their informality explains why they have become forever associated with academics and

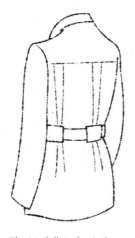

The Norfolk jacket is the ancestor of the sports jacket

writers and other nonconformists, who through the 1940s and 50s were loath to appear "dressed-up" and yet had to follow the convention of wearing at least a jacket in public.

There is great mystique around tweed, largely due to the marketing efforts of the British textile industry in the interwar years. Tweed is made of carded, short-fibre wool, which gives it a rough texture that evokes the whole romance of the English countryside, of hunting and shooting and shivering in draughty stone castles.

The word itself does not originate, as is commonly thought, from the River Tweed, which divides England and Scotland, but comes from the Scottish word *tweel*, for a particular kind of handwoven cloth.

The best-known brand name is Harris Tweed, the only fully handwoven tweed that is commercially produced. It is entirely made by islanders – woven, dyed, and finished – on the remote Scottish islands of Lewis, Harris, Uist, and Barra, in the Outer Hebrides. So strict is this definition that an actual act of the British Parliament was passed in 1993 to create a Harris Tweed Authority, and to ensure that all fabrics bearing the Harris Tweed trademark – an orb with a cross on top – are made here and in the traditional manner.

There is an intriguing subtlety to the patterns and colours found in these highly textured cloths, and much has been made of their resemblance to the natural landscape of the British Isles – especially since so many of the dyes used in their colouring once came from local plants, roots, lichen, and seaweed. "There is a lovely smell with tweed," wrote the Welsh novelist Richard Llewellyn in *How Green Was My Valley*. "Good and honest, of the earth and humankind. . . . I had a brown tweed, the colour of a ploughed field in the pebbly soil."

That about sums up both the joy and the drawback of such traditional men's apparel: those who find this description attractive are probably not fanatics of Japanese design and German electronica. This lovely description captures precisely what makes peaty colours and rough fabrics so romantic, and so unhip.

Now, of course, the sports jacket is no longer necessarily made of tweed. When the Italians got involved in making sports jackets, they turned them into much lighter garments, often made of varying proportions of high-twist wool, cashmere, silk, or linen. Italian jackets are often textured and patterned to look like tweed – in herringbones, cheviots, or houndstooths – but they feel more like suit jackets.

And this has in turn made them more attractive to the younger set. Square can be cultivated; square means Old World, which can be sexy. Picture the actor James Gandolfini, as Tony Soprano, threatening to disembowel somebody – in a soft brown jacket with a yellowish silk pocket square. The last thing he looks is nerdy. The pocket square is the thing that really puts it over the edge: it's what makes the sports jacket more sensual than paternal.

A soft wool and cashmere jacket, with charcoal trousers, a spread-collar shirt, a silk tie, and a pocket square, will make you look European: the younger you are, the more daring you will look. Women will reach across restaurant tables just to stroke the fabric. And you can wear more-colourful shoes than you can with a dark suit: burgundy brogues or brown slip-ons.

However, if you pair the sports jacket with a polo shirt, or with loafers or deck shoes – the standard casual Friday uniform of provincial America – then you won't look sexy at all; you will look like a dad.

The Advanced Class will also consider all sorts of hybrids, such as a jacket which is a cross between a sports jacket and a coat, a smock-like thing like a lengthened golf jacket. Japanese designers in particular, such as Comme des Garçons and Yohji Yamamoto, have made beautiful, light, hip-length coats with four or five buttons that close very high. Recently, Giorgio Armani sold a sweater in the shape of a sports jacket: it was in stretchy, cable-knit wool, but cut like a slim 1920s tweed jacket. These variants are great substitutes for sports jackets in artistic enterprises, or for the upscale casual event that requires style but not stuffiness.

The golf jacket

If you have a lot of sexy fitted sports shirts, which you will wear untucked, you may consider a very casual but stylish option for covering them: the golf jacket. Note that it is not a bomber jacket: the bomber is gathered at the waist. This is all straight lines. It can be worn indoors or out. It may have a small collar, or none; it may also have patch pockets on the chest. You may call this an Eisenhower jacket, after a particularly successful and gentlemanly general of that name; if you have more humble ambitions, you may call it the Gas Station Attendant. Whatever the nomenclature, this item is useful for projecting boyish nonchalance. To avoid looking like an actual golfer, match it only with funky clothes – narrow trousers or jeans, not pleated khakis – and don't buy it in light colours. And, unless you really are in a grunge band, unstitch the name tag that says "Larry."

Socks

The discussion of socks comes, here, at the end of suits and jackets, because it is with dressy outfits that the choice of socks becomes the most important.

Socks may be more expressive than grey or black.

It is only, in fact, since the invention of the trouser (not adopted by men in all classes of European society until the mid-1800s) that socks have become invisible. In the middle ages, men wore bare legs under skirts, tunics, and robes, or tightly fitted cloth leggings, sometimes made of strips of cloth wrapped around the leg. Knitted cloth, and in particular silks, were available only to the aristocracy. All the great Renaissance portraits of gentlemen in embroidered robes and elegant legs in tights are of the fabulously wealthy. Think of the famous Holbein portrait of Henry VIII, with his strong legs in a wide stance: this painting is as much about the extravagant clothes, including fine hosiery, as it is about the man.

Right through the eighteenth and nineteenth centuries, hosiery was a mark of privilege. When a lower-class mob stormed the Bastille in 1789, they became known as the *"sans-culottes"* – not because, as it is widely believed, they had no pants, but because they wore loose trousers, instead of knee breeches (*"culottes"*) with hose. In fact, *"les sans-culottes"* could be more accurately called *"les sans-bas"* (the tightless).

But the victory of the underclass in the French Revolution was an important step in the democratization of fashion, which began the inexorable trend toward sombre colour, plain texture, and the loose covering of the body – the rise of bourgeois fashion representing the political victory of that class.

When early-nineteenth-century British dandies such as Beau Brummell went out in society, they wore knee breeches and stockings, so the finery of their stockings was very much on display. But by around 1850, even the British upper classes were being seen in long trousers. They were very tight-fitting trousers, by our standards, but they still rendered flashy hosiery invisible and therefore unnecessary.

All this to say that elegant socks have a fine and important pedigree, and one need not be afraid of them. Europeans are still more daring in their hosiery than we coarse New Worlders. I remember a visiting French professor at my university who lectured us (on Rousseau) wearing loafers with a very low vamp and socks so sheer they could only be described as pantyhose. You could see the veins in his foot through them. The class was so stunned by this apparent cross-dressing that we stared at his feet for the duration of his lectures, to the detriment of Rousseau.

This daintiness is perhaps a little too daring for the North American business environment, but it does at least show that there is more to life than grey

"Elegant SOCKS have a FINE and important PEDIGREE, and one need not be AFRAID of them."

and black. The Advanced Class will wear socks that are a shade lighter than their trousers, and consider how their socks match their shirt or their tie. (Note that the odd glimpse as you cross your legs is all we want to see of your socks, and we particularly don't want to see a strip of naked flesh where the sock ends. Make sure your socks are long enough to prevent this.) Fred Astaire wore white socks with slipper-like loafers, presumably to draw attention to his nimble feet; Cary Grant was said to wear his trademark champagne colour with every outfit he owned. Why not lighten up a little? The brief flash of an interesting colour between cuff and leather is a sign of eccentricity or artsiness; like the pocket square and the tie, it is one of our all-too-few channels of artistic expression.

Not too interesting a colour, of course: bright red always looks goofy, and loud patterns or logos are never done. (Socks that say "CK" are in particular to be abhorred; readers of this book are not walking advertising billboards.) But I have worn dark purple with a navy suit, to much female admiration; I have also had success with dove grey and salmon pink. Salmon socks are, like a bright rose in one's lapel or a white silk scarf with one's overcoat, a secret homage to the *ancien régime*.

CHAPTER FOUR

SHIRTS

Society, which the more I think of it
astonishes me the more, is founded upon cloth.
– THOMAS CARLYLE

n Beau Brummell's day – and indeed, in some classes right up until the twentieth century – shirts were considered a form of underclothing. They were made of fine linen until the middle of the nineteenth century, when cotton took over – both textiles being suitable because they are comfortable against the skin and absorbent. Brummell's shirts didn't have buttons, either – you pulled them over your head. The only parts of the shirt you could politely show in public were the collar and the cuffs, protruding slightly from under a jacket. These two elements have always been areas for dandyish display, ever since European aristocrats of the Renaissance showed off lace collars and cuffs.

The white shirt has proved such a mainstay because it has always been a mark of privilege: you can't keep white cotton clean if you're performing manual labour. White cuffs and collars in particular are impractical if you're milking cows or mining coal; working men wore coloured shirts, often with no collar at all.

The first mass-produced shirt with buttons all the way down the front was a product of the British firm Brown and Company; they registered the design in 1871 (although they were being worn before that). Shirts with detachable collars and cuffs were actually an American invention, dating from around 1820; detachable collars continued to be popular in Europe and America until the First World War, when government-issued uniforms accustomed millions of men to the wearing of soft, attached collars.

By 1910, the British humorist P.G. Wodehouse could use scorn toward detachable cuffs as a mark of class snobbery. In *Psmith in the City*, his idle and elegant character Psmith, who wears a monocle and lavender gloves, is forced, like so many of us, to enter the dusty world of commerce. At the bank where he takes dull employment, he must endure his colleague Bristow, who takes off his shirt cuffs when beginning work and stacks them "in a glistening pile" on his desk. This harrows Psmith's sensitive soul, for "It was part of Psmith's philosophy that a man who wore detachable cuffs had passed beyond the limits of human toleration." Psmith's disdain for Bristow comes mostly from Bristow's refusal to be elegant at work – his treating of the office as some kind of grim factory floor on which one's appearance doesn't matter.

Our modern equivalent of the detachable cuff is the coloured dress shirt with contrasting white collar and cuffs. I know this look is popular with an older crowd, and reputable shops sell it. But to me it will forever provoke the image of a red-faced guy with a phallic car, a big cigar, and a big ring. The word *snazzy* comes to mind. (If this is an idea you find glamorous, by all means cultivate the look; I am betraying prejudices here.)

This sort of flash is for some reason popular with television sports newscasters, who have lately been committing even fouler outrages with odd vertical stripes or zigzags on their shirt collars. This is beyond snazzy; it moves you into the terrain of *swanky*. It is a pro-athlete-at-awards-ceremony aesthetic, sported by men who want to be seen as rebels. This is like keeping a short haircut but growing a little rat-tail at the back: daring in a conservative environment, perhaps, but hideous.

It is difficult to explain what makes any innovation cheesy as opposed to expressive. Perhaps it's the combination of business conservatism and frat-boy colour – like jokey motifs on bright suspenders – that makes me squirm. If you want to look unconventional, skip the dress shirt altogether. Wear PVC or chain mail and I am intrigued; flashy shirt collars turn me into a stony conservative.

> "The COLOURED dress shirt with CONTRASTING white COLLAR and CUFFS is beyond SNAZZY; it moves you into the terrain of *SWANKY*."

It is the combination of the proletarian and the overly formal that offends the sensitive Psmith, too: "In addition, Bristow wore a small black moustache and a ring and that, as Psmith informed Mike, put the lid on it."

Fit

Too many men have had their necks measured only once. When they were fourteen, their fathers took them for a ritual first set of grown-up purchases at Fit-Rite Clothiers. Did this not happen to you? The tailor snapped a tape around your neck, pronounced you a 15½, and that's what you've always been.

No wonder dressing in grown-up clothes is so often called uncomfortable. Men who denounce suits like to claim that they can't wear ties because they are an unbearable restraint on their breathing and swallowing. This is nonsense: you can tie a tie as tightly or as loosely as you desire. The problem, of which these men are unaware, is not the tie, but the shirt collar. These guys are wearing their shirts too small. Many, if not most, men do. If you can't wait to loosen your tie and unbutton your shirt collar as soon as you step out of the office, then you are one of them.

Cotton shirt collars are cut about a half-inch bigger than they say they are, to make up for the inevitable shrinking of cotton when washed. In other words, a 16½ is usually actually a 17. And even this, I find, is not enough to make up for shrinkage.

A good salesman knows this and will measure your neck leaving space for one finger between the tape and your skin. (Furthermore, your size will change as you age: you should get measured at least once every couple of years.)

But I go further. I buy my shirts a half inch larger than even the good salesman tells me to. (I am a 15½; I buy a 16.) They argue with me quite sternly. I am firm. And I never regret it. Yes, on first wearing the collar is too big. (The danger of wearing a collar that's too loose is that the tie will cause it to buckle and for the two points to overlap where they meet.) Wash it once and it fits.

You want your collar to protrude just over a centimetre above the back of your jacket. You want your shirt cuffs to protrude the same amount beyond your jacket cuff. Don't be afraid to have your shirt sleeves cut too long: you can always button the cuffs tightly enough to stop them from sliding over your hands. In fact, they should be that tight.

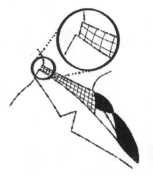

Your shirt collar should protrude about one centimetre above your jacket

Quality

There are few sartorial pleasures more sensual than slipping on a crisply pressed, fine dress shirt. Shirts – particularly those with French cuffs, for cufflinks rather than buttons – can make you feel much richer than you are. Maseratis and Greek islands may be forever inaccessible to most of us, but we can all experience genuine luxury for the price of one shirt. Heavy, stiff cuffs finish the sleeve; cufflinks add a spark of hedonism, a glint of abandon hiding behind the cotton and wool.

If the cotton is soft and the fit not constricting, a dress shirt is also the most comfortable garment in the conventional wardrobe.

How to spot the best cotton? You will see boastful labels advertising various numbers and phrases. "Ply" refers to the yarn: if two strands are twisted together to make a single fibre, the yarn is two-ply. There are fabrics with up to six strands in each thread, but in cotton shirts, two-ply is better than most and is generally an indication of quality. The thread count may also be listed: the higher the thread count, the finer the yarn and the more luxurious the fabric. An "80s" shirt means that there are eighty threads per inch. If it says 80/2, it means eighty two-ply threads. This will be a nice one, but very good dress shirts are made with fabric that contains 140 threads per square inch; the best shirts go up to 220.

You might see the phrase "**single-needle tailoring.**" Some machines use two parallel needles to sew seams; a better-quality shirt is made with a single needle which goes back and sews another line very close to its first line. This takes twice as much time. You can recognize single-needle tailoring when only one line of stitching is visible on the outside of the seam, or when the two lines of stitching on the seams are very close together. The advantage of this procedure is supposed to be that it is more accurate, and will thus produce a seam which puckers less. In reality, it is desirable simply because it is more expensive. Very few ready-made shirts are sewn with single needles. So don't worry about it.

In any good dress shirt you will want **removable collar stays**. These are the small tabs of plastic that fit into slots sewn underneath the points of the collar. The collar stay keeps the points flat, not curled inward, and weighs the points of the collar down, ensuring that they stay touching the shirt front and tucked under the jacket's lapels (if they are long points) at all times. You can buy brass collar stays in different sizes at old-fashioned and expensive men's clothing stores – they cost between ten and twenty dollars, and are better than plastic because . . . well, for no good reason, really. They're just nicer to handle and won't melt if you accidentally iron your shirt with them in.

If you are going for the very best – say you can afford custom-made shirts, or for the top end of ready-made shirts such as those found on Jermyn Street in London – you will want to consider these other indications of quality:

- Look for a **split yoke**. The yoke is the top panel of the back of the shirt. If it has a vertical seam that divides it in two, it will probably cost almost twice as much as any other shirt you own. The point of the split yoke is ostensibly to permit alterations that take into account shoulders of

A split yoke is a sign of quality

different heights, but, as with all these signs of fastidiousness, it is in effect nothing more than a symbol of labour.

- **Patterns will be matched** at the seams. That is to say that the lines of stripes or checks will be perfectly lined up – especially at the aforementioned split in the yoke.
- At the bottom of the side seams, where the tail of the shirt meets the front, there will be a small triangle of reinforcing material, usually thicker than the rest of the shirt's cotton. This is called a **gusset** and serves to prevent tearing.
- Look for **several pleats** where the sleeve meets the cuff. Again, these are useless indicators of painstaking labour.
- **Mother-of-pearl** buttons look exactly like plastic ones unless you are peering closely – but mother-of-pearl buttons are so hard they will shatter the needle of a sewing machine. They are a secret luxury no one will recognize but you.
- The vent in the sleeve, above where the cuff buttons, is called a **sleeve placket**. It should have a functioning button. The best shirts will have a *horizontal buttonhole on the sleeve placket*. This proves that the buttonhole is hand-sewn, because it must be more precisely placed than a vertical buttonhole. Truly useless labour; truly expensive shirt.

But as with all other clothes, quality means nothing if it doesn't make you look good. The most

"QUALITY means NOTHING if it doesn't make you look GOOD."

important part of the shirt, the part that defines its style, its character, is the collar.

Collars

The thing that differentiates a collar the most is not just its width – that is to say, the length of the points – but the degree to which the points are separated, the angle in other words on which they are cut. This angle determines the degree to which the collar is **spread**. The greater the spread, the flashier, and more dressy, the shirt. A very widely spread collar is also called a **cutaway**. A longer collar is said to have **straight points**.

Spread collar (below) and straight-pointed

Straight points means a pointy collar. These can be short, medium, or long. (Same goes for cutaway collars: there are wide variations in the length of the points.)

Long straight-point collars became fashionable in the 1930s and 40s: you can see photographs of American icons Fred Astaire and Clark Gable looking natty in them. In the 1950s, as sobriety began to dominate masculine sartorial values across the Western world, collars shrank again, to a conservative compromise: medium-spread, medium length. And then they swelled, massively and grotesquely, in the late sixties and seventies, until they were silly flapping sheets . . . only to shrink again in the 1980s, into tiny little bands. The pendulum seems to have stopped swinging so excessively, for the time being: all of these extremes are seen as unflattering now. Very narrow collars do little for a long neck or for a wide face; fashionable shirts today have collars with points just long enough to disappear under the jacket's lapel.

The choice between straight point and spread collar is a personal one. Other guidebooks will give you diagrams of various facial types with hints on which collar is appropriate for you (wide faces should stick to pointy collars, thin faces to spreads, etc.), which I never find convincing: your face will stay the same shape regardless of your collar. So pick the style you like.

"The CHOICE between STRAIGHT point and SPREAD collar is a PERSONAL one. So pick the STYLE you LIKE."

My personal tastes tend toward a moderate cutaway. It's a British look. Notice how assured, debonair, and relaxed Prince Charles looks, even in a conservative double-breasted suit: it's all in the shirt collar, which he wears invariably spread. The long straight-point looks too restrained to me; it looks somehow tight. Not to mention a little, well, nineties.

And it covers so much of your tie knot. Ties are beautiful things and should not be retiring or shy.

Don't go overboard with the cutaway collar. Very widely spread collars are definitely dandy terrain, with a touch of the Continent about them. They also necessitate some attention to the kind of tie knot you use. The collar frames the tie knot: all it should reveal is the knot itself, not the two ends of the tie going under your collar. The wider the spread, the wider the knot you will want to tie. Very few collars

The collar should frame the tie knot

are so widely spread as to demand a full Windsor knot; a half Windsor will do. (We will attack the various knots in detail in the next chapter.)

Here are a handful of other collar styles. I describe them for your entertainment only, for I am not fond of any of them.

The **"Eton"** or **"club"** collar is the little rounded one you see in photos from the 1930s. It derives from schoolboy uniforms and makes you look twelve. Often worn by guys who want to proclaim some nostalgia, or to be seen as nonconformist or eccentric. I find it rather sexless.

The **pin** collar has two holes in it, which hold a horizontal metal bar, usually gold.

A similar idea is behind the **tab** collar. This has a band of fabric which snaps or buttons underneath the tie's knot. Like the pin collar, it looks tight and fussy.

Then there is the **button-down** collar, a favourite of Americans, university professors, and newspapermen, which connects the collar points to the shirt by means of two small buttons. It was made famous by Brooks Brothers, and so is often thought of as a Brooks Brothers collar. I think it is popular in academic and preppy circles because it looks casual: visible buttons look functional and therefore practical; they are the opposite of finery and delicacy. The kind of man who wears a button-down collar doesn't want to project any kind of pretension or effeminacy. He wants to be seen as a down-to-earth guy, not an elitist of any kind. I needn't

You will notice that young people are imposing a different definition of this phrase. To anyone under thirty, "button-down" means not a kind of collar but a kind of shirt – a shirt with buttons, as opposed to a T-shirt. In other words, what we call simply a shirt. This lexical drift is sociologically interesting: it indicates just how obsolescent this entire discussion is. When you need a special term to describe a shirt with buttons, you know that the T-shirt has become the norm. Readers of this book are encouraged to resist this vocabulary shift for as long as they can. ☙

explain, by now, that I personally have no affinity for these sensitivities. I don't understand the point of the button-down collar whatsoever. It looks like a weekend sports shirt, as if it should be matched with pleated khaki cotton trousers and outdoorsy brown shoes (with heavily lugged eyelets). These collars may be tolerated with tweed jackets. With fine suits, they are too casual.

No, honestly, I must confess I disdain button-down collars even with sports jackets or blazers, or at any time – they're just so minivan-weekendy, so ripe with connotations of barbecues and deck shoes, so *prim*.

Finally, we descend to the lowest level of tacky-collar hell: the **collarless** shirt, the one with a narrow band around the neck and no turndown. This Amish Farmer look was dear to hippies who loved its suggestion of rural life, and was then adopted by minimalist Japanese designers in the 1980s. It is now seriously unhip – or worse, sexless. You might as well wear a sign that says Earnest Boomer – or Sportscaster, the guy who is daringly dressed in avant-garde looks of ten years ago.

Colours

In the 1950s, conservative Americans believed that white was the only colour of shirt a gentleman could wear with a suit after 6 p.m. Mercifully, that stricture has eased. However, white is still the most formal colour: it is what men tend to wear at important occasions – weddings, funerals, addressing the United Nations. White is also the most conservative colour, which means that it is a little dull. Its popularity, even for ceremonious events, is fading. It can still look extremely impressive, particularly with an austere tie – grey, black, or silver – against a dark charcoal suit.

Blue is more flattering for most men, and it's easy to match with almost every colour. Most North Americans are nervous about the very bright blue shirts that European men wear, and they shouldn't be. Bold is beautiful.

And let's not avoid the subject of the other colours magazines and department stores display every spring. Admit it: you're a little afraid of them. You have seen the rows of pastel shirts in the department stores, all pretty for spring, with their dazzling ties in outrageous acid green and electric blue; you have seen the striped ties on checked shirts or dotty ties on stripy shirts, and you are afraid. The current vogue for bright shirts and bright ties is stunning, when they are arranged like beds of flowers on tabletops or in magazines, but can you see yourself wearing clothing so pretty it looks edible?

And so much of it is, well, frankly, pink.

Don't be alarmed; pink is big and it is manly. It always has been. British men so conservative they brush their teeth with Scotch have been wearing

"WHITE is the most CONSERVATIVE colour, which means that it is a little DULL."

bright or pale pink shirts since the invention of umbrellas. They wear them with high-contrast pin-striped suits and florid ties and pocket squares and cufflinks and they look so intimidatingly masculine, you'd think they ran an Empire. I swear, these guys are so square they are afraid to part their hair on the right.

By coincidence, one of the most famous Jermyn Street shirtmakers is called Thomas Pink. If you buy a shirt there, you take it away in a gorgeous pink bag or box with the word PINK emblazoned on it; this does a lot to rehabilitate the colour in the masculine world. The fact that they cost hundreds of pounds makes them even more power-friendly.

Admittedly, pink shirts have had a few troubling associations. In the seventies and eighties, the pink shirt was the badge of the East Coast preppy or the frat boy, inevitably accompanied by khaki chinos and deck shoes. (Think of the oxford-cloth, button-down, Ralph-Lauren-style shirt, open and untucked, over a polo shirt. This is not what we are recommending.) At this time it was, just like the Jermyn Street shirt, an appurtenance of social class – but without the dandy touch. Guys who did not belong to that class – meaning most guys – would have been horrified nevertheless at the idea of wearing pink. Pink was for girls (or worse).

That era is over. The North American male is becoming more sophisticated, less preppy. English actors and politicians help, of course – note British prime minister Tony Blair, who has a penchant for pastel colours and massive military force. Chicks love these guys.

Pink is flexible, too: it matches navy, light grey, and charcoal suits, and accentuates silver, blue, yellow, bright green, and (depending on the shade) purple in ties. Another fun trick is to try to match another shade of pink to the shirt – in the tie or in the pocket square. This is daring – Advanced Class only – but you'd be surprised at how well it works.

Very dark shirts – navy, charcoal, black – can look a little mobstery, particularly with lighter-coloured ties. This tone-on-tone look of the nineties (popularized by game- and talk-show host Regis Philbin) has faded in popularity.

Patterns

The big development in shirts in the past couple of years has been the return of pattern. Stripes and checks are back, and they are being matched with striped suits and striped ties, contributing to a more textured look.

Like all such things, checks and plaids go through cycles of modishness. Their current ascendancy is interesting, considering their stuffy past. Plaids gained a foothold in men's clothing in the 1840s, a trend sparked by Queen Victoria, whose favourite home was at Balmoral in Scotland. Scottish land-owners of the time had been gradually refining their traditional loud tartans to more subdued checks, in

"STRIPES and CHECKS are back, and they are being MATCHED with striped SUITS and striped TIES."

an effort to seem more urbane (and possibly less warlike, for tartan is tribal). Victoria's consort, Prince Albert, wore Scottish checks and plaids back to London, where his rural style was aped by social-climbing gentlemen eager to appear royal or at least estate-owning.

It's paradoxical that we have come to think of loud plaids as déclassé (owing, no doubt, to American golf-wear excesses of the 1970s), for right through the 1930s, snobs such as Evelyn Waugh could wear loud, even garish check wool suits and still be projecting a fundamental conservatism. And now, after the 1990s – a decade of minimalist solids in shirts and ties – the most expensive and trendy shirts may well have a pattern of small squares, often made with two colours (horizontal lines of one colour, vertical of another). Which brings us to one more English story.

There was, in the late eighteenth century, an English horseman named Tattersall. He died in 1795 and gave his name to a London auction room where racehorses were bought and sold. Through the strange evolution of language, his name is now solely associated with exactly this check pattern of small open squares, a little over a centimetre on each side, made of stripes of one colour or two. It is usually found on rougher, oxford-cloth shirts, for wear with tweed jackets, wool ties, heavy brogues, green Barbour raincoats, shotguns, and Land Rovers, because – like the various patterns of Scottish tweeds

– it is a connoter of land and horse ownership. In fact, the name derives from the patterns used in wool horse blankets in those famous auction rooms. The English gentleman often wears tattersalls in quite loud combinations of colours – in the country or at the track, not in the city.

But the tattersall check has recently undergone a transformation. As demand for interesting colours grows, so does demand for texture. Checked and striped shirts of all kinds are suddenly back, everywhere, and not just with tweed jackets. Subtle tattersall checks – say, plain white squares on a blue background, or pale purple on white – are showing up on fine cotton shirts with elegant dark suits and cufflinks. Daring men are matching palely striped shirts – with stripes of varying widths and colours – with patterned ties and pinstripe or nailhead check suits, for a complicated effect that wreaks havoc on video broadcasts.

It is nerve-racking, I know, to attempt to match a striped shirt with a striped suit with a striped tie, particularly if the colours are all different (as they must be). The key is to ensure that the patterns are of notably different widths on all the elements, to ensure contrast: try a chalkstripe suit, with faint lines, over a shirt with a bold, bright stripe that is much narrower. The tie's stripes are diagonal (and they may be irregular as well), so they will look separate. A striped pocket square, at this point, would be over the top.

"Subtle TATTERSALL checks are showing up on fine COTTON SHIRTS with elegant DARK SUITS and CUFFLINKS."

Texture

Sea Island cotton, a cotton of very long strands, originally grown off the southeastern coast of the United States and now cultivated in the Caribbean, can be so fine it is mistaken for silk. Other long-strand cottons, such as Egyptian cotton, or the American Pima cotton (marketed as Supima, which is a trade name), can be equally fine. The weave also determines the texture: the coarse weave you remember from schoolboy shirts is called an oxford weave. I am not a huge fan of oxford cloth, myself, unless it is the luxurious blend of cotton and wool made by the British company Viyella, usually for soft casual shirts in plaid or tattersall checks.

With the advanced weaving technology now used around the world, it is possible to have shirts of extremely fine cotton that also have a palpable texture. Indeed, texture is resurgent: shirts with faint ribs or waffles, which for a while I associated with polyester blends from the seventies, now seem quite luxurious – and they can enliven the very dressy white shirt, make it not so square. A gauzy white shirt with a subtle waffle texture (something like a **piqué** or **marcella** texture, terms we will address in the chapter on formal wear) can look extremely elegant.

"Texture is RESURGENT: shirts with faint RIBS or WAFFLES can ENLIVEN the very DRESSY white shirt."

Other Details

Most dress shirts will have one or two **pleats** in the back panel. Their function is largely aesthetic: they puff out the back of the shirt so that it does not cling to you and contributes to your overall manly silhouette – with shoulders bigger than your waist. So pleats are generally a good thing.

There are two kinds of pleats: the **centre**, or **box**, pleat, and the two **side** pleats. The box pleat is fuller, adds more volume, or body, to the shirt. It is also slightly less formal; it tends to be associated with oxford-cloth shirts. The side or double pleat, one over each shoulder blade, is a little more subtle and looks a little more dressy. But these are secret details which no one but you is going to appreciate (since you're keeping your jacket on most of the time anyway, right?), so don't worry.

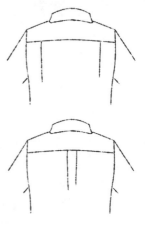

Side pleats (top) and centre, or box, pleats

The other thing you don't have to worry about is the breast pocket on the shirt. Some good shirts have them; some don't. I have always been baffled as to what such a pocket could possibly be used for.

Another truly useless detail is the monogram. Tailors who make you custom shirts will suggest that the monogram is an emblem of true class – they will show you pictures of Hollywood stars from the forties with their initials embroidered on their cuffs, their chests, everywhere. Besides (the tailor will add in a lowered voice), the monogram will let everyone know that you've had the shirt made for you – it will be a sign of your purchasing power.

To which you should answer, All the more reason to avoid it. The visible monogram is the opposite of classy: it is brash and vain. The guy who likes to put

A tip for the cash-strapped

A beautiful shirt and tie can save you a lot of money. People will notice them, particularly if they are bold, *before they notice your suit.* So if your suit is inexpensive, your shirt and tie can make up for it. ❧

his initials all over his clothing is the same kind of guy who likes those blue shirts with white collar and cuffs: a guy who always orders the biggest cigar and the oldest brandy. Needless to say, he talks the loudest, too.

Some readers – fans of *The Sopranos*, maybe, and of Donald Trump – may find this image of the alpha male romantic, and don't let me keep you from your aspirations. But if you absolutely must have your shirts monogrammed – because your grandfather did it and you feel nostalgic about it or something – put your initials in an invisible place, not on the shirt cuff. Put it on your breast pocket – and then never take your jacket off.

The Custom Shirt

Like any other item of clothing, the shirt can be custom-tailored. The point is not so much the fit: most of your shirt is usually hidden, so the neck and sleeve size are what really matter, and most combinations of neck and sleeve measurements are available at every department store. The advantage of the tailored shirt is often, believe it or not, the price: it can be just as inexpensive to have a bunch of shirts made to measure as it is to buy them off the rack – particularly if you have a Hong Kong connection.

I suspect, too, that the guys who make appointments with one or other of the Hong Kong shirtmakers who visit most large cities regularly tend to do so in groups, as a partly social event; there is a pleasure in the ritual itself.

The tailor books a suite in a hotel for a day or two, where he sets up an assembly line of measurers as his clientele files through. Client selects a fabric from a book of swatches, chooses collar and cuff style, and orders a minimum of three shirts. Clients then go out for beers together, having enjoyed a uniquely masculine pleasure, and perhaps subconsciously feeling that the world of business will remain a stable and reassuring place only as long as words like *tailor* and *swatch* remain in common parlance. Tailor then returns to Hong Kong, where cotton is in large supply and labour is cheap, and client receives three shirts by mail in about four months' time.

The risks are numerous. If tailor disappears in the interim, with client's deposit, and shirts do not materialize, he will be difficult to track down. (I'm not suggesting this happens often, but the men who buy shirts this way tend to be businessmen, and they are aware of the possibility.) And if, when the shirt arrives, the fit is not perfect or the colour not what one imagined, to send it back and wait another half a year to see if the problem is corrected seems like a great deal of effort.

There are of course tailors with shops right in your own town who will make a shirt of which each piece is individually cut for you (unlike some, who simply modify existing shapes), out of two-ply by 100s cotton from English and Italian mills. But this will set you back at least two hundred dollars a piece.

For many power-brokers, the advantage of the bespoke shirt is simply in the convenience and ego boost of having a tailor come to your office and measure you. I knew a stockbroker whose boss used to have his shirt measurements taken in his glass-walled office, in full view of his staff. There he was, the bare-chested emperor, conquering continents on the phone, proudly oblivious to the factotums buzzing about him with their tape measures. Like Nero bathing in public, like Louis XIV, whose daily toilet was an event to which only the most privileged courtiers were invited, this boss knew the value of a physical presence. You see, there is so much more to fashion than just fashion.

"In the ABSENCE of ties at EVERYDAY social events SHIRTS have become quite FLASHY."

The Sports Shirt

It has been said that shirts are the new ties. In other words, in an age of increasingly casual dressing, your shirt can do double duty: it is the focal point of your outfit, not a mere backdrop. In the absence of ties at everyday social events – cocktail parties, after-work drinks, brunch – shirts have become quite flashy.

The modern sports shirt is no longer the button-down corduroy thing that you used to wear to barbecues with khaki pants. Nor is it a baggy cotton thing with two breast pockets with flaps over them (the shirt that tries to say: I am part cowboy and part war photographer).

Polo shirts, although still useful for events at which you don't want to stand out but don't want to wear a tie either, are also on their way out. (Particularly those frightening multicoloured ones – you know the machine-patterned ones that you get in golf stores? Avoid them at all times.)

The new sports shirt requires a certain level of fitness, because it is fitted (that is, it has darts sewn into it). It clings to the waist and extends below it, untucked. It comes in all kinds of fabrics: in cotton, in rayon (a natural fibre which is soft, thin, faintly shiny and clingy), in cotton-polyester blends. Yes, they look a little seventies. But do not be afraid of these blends: they give a shirt a sheen, and they hold bright colours well without fading. The sexy sports shirt is the kind of thing you have seen young, pumped bartenders wearing. It has some kind of pattern on it: bold stripes, big squares, or random flowers. It has big cuffs, which you fold back only once, so they move a little as you shake martinis.

Even if you have moved on from the bartending stage of your life, who doesn't want the social and – let's be honest – sexual power of the guy pouring drinks?

This is the shirt you wear with a black blazer and jeans, or with a fashion-forward black suit.

> "The NEW sports shirt CLINGS to the WAIST and extends below it, UNTUCKED."

Even with a suit, you don't tuck it in. And let the cuffs protrude lavishly and loosely from your jacket sleeves. (Obviously, this advice will be taken hesitantly by those over forty.)

CHAPTER FIVE

TIES

If only to go warm were gorgeous,
Why, nature needs not what thou gorgeous wear'st,
Which scarcely keeps thee warm.
– WILLIAM SHAKESPEARE

The necktie, once called a **cravat,** evolved from a simple scarf which kept the collar closed and the neck warm. The word comes from the French *cravate*, which has an interesting derivation. The French king Louis XIII hired some Croatian cavalrymen as mercenaries during the Thirty Years' War and was impressed by the debonair and complicated way in which they knotted their scarves. This elaborate knot became the fashion in the king's court, and was a *Hrvat*, which is "Croat" in Croatian. *Hrvat* became corrupted to *cravate* in French. So what you are really wearing with your suit is not a tie but a Croatian.

The cravat was often tied, well into the nineteenth century, around a **stock,** which was a high, stiff collar of military origin. The stock had a fancy

knot in front of it. So "stock" came to be a syno-
nym, in nineteenth-century Britain, for the scarf or
cravat itself.

In Beau Brummell's age, the neck scarf – either a
stock or cravat – was the focal point of male high
fashion: it was the product of careful daily labour
and left its wearer barely able to turn his head. The
most famous story about Brummell is that a caller
found him in his dressing room with his valet in
the middle of the morning, surrounded by a pile
of rumpled muslin strands. "Those," explained
Brummell, "are our failures."

There are mocking caricatures from the popular
press of the time which show men's faces quite disappeared into their collars, and apparently they
were hardly exaggerated: some dandies wore their
collar points up to their cheekbones. Brummell
himself would wrap a stiff vertical collar, about a
foot high, around his head and face, then fold it
down once. With his chin now pointed at the ceiling,
he proceeded to wrap around the collar a lightly
starched cloth, also about a foot long. He then stood
in front of a mirror and very slowly pushed his chin
downward, achieving the perfect creasing of the
collar and rumpling of the scarf.

So we can hardly complain about the discomfort
of the modern tie.

In the Romantic era, the middle of the nineteenth
century, cravats grew looser and more scarf-like,
particularly among those who wanted to follow the

"In BEAU BRUMMELL'S age, the NECK SCARF was the FOCAL point of male high FASHION."

sudden vogue for "artistic" dress; painters and poets were wearing fulminant peasant-like neckerchiefs rather than carefully knotted ties. I mention these shifts only to show that fashion has not, as one would think, grown inexorably more casual and comfortable over the course of human history; it goes through cycles of restriction and relaxation (which inevitably mirror social and political shifts). The Romantic collar was probably looser than the contemporary one; it grew stiff and tight again at the end of the century, when respectability and humility became the dominant social values they still are today.

Until this point, there was little distinction between bow ties and other kinds of knots. The bow tie that had its ends hidden, as opposed to draped over the chest, started to appear in the 1870s. It became firmly associated in the 1880s with formal wear – particularly with white shirts and black frock coats with tails.

Nowadays, the tie is merely decorative, and as such, it may be argued, is utterly useless. Indeed, there was quite a flutter of media excitement in 1998 when a Dutch prince made a big deal about refusing to wear one. In a speech opening a show of African fashion, seventy-three-year-old Prince Claus of the Netherlands angrily tore off his tie, threw it at the feet of his queen, Beatrix, and denounced it as a "snake" around his neck. The media in the Netherlands were thrilled: a TV anchorman who

Reps and regimentals

There have long been very complicated discussions in men's fashion books and magazines about the correct name for certain kinds of striped ties – Americans call them reps, a word for the kind of weave that produces their corded or ribbed surface, apparently from old French – and about the correct angle and direction for the tilt of the stripes. But these discussions are increasingly academic. The reason for all the consternation was that there is a long-standing British tradition of wearing one's military and sporting associations on one's tie, and that these particularly associative ties are, for a certain British class, almost sacred. If you belong to a certain regiment or went to a certain school, you may, according to this class, wear the tie which signals your belonging; if you wear it without ☞

reported the story that evening also ripped off his tie, on air, and subsequent reports credited the prince with starting a trend they called "Claustrophilia."

The American media, ever eager for evidence of their own earnest populism, were even more thrilled, and gleefully predicted a drop in tie sales. They quoted scores of middle-management businessmen who denounced the tie as oppressive and boring.

The problem with these reports was not that they were inaccurate, but that they were so far behind the times as to be confusing. Men stopped wearing ties en masse during the social upheaval of the 1960s. Perhaps the prince spent this period trapped in his palace. (Watch, European aristocrats will be proclaiming the value of popular music next.)

The open-neck shirt was the innovation of the youthful baby boomers – the same people who now hold every position of authority. Now, very few men anywhere have jobs that force them to wear ties. Ties are rarely worn to private social functions or even for television appearances; they are avoided in the domains of publishing, media, education, and science. I know accountants, doctors, even lawyers who do not wear ties to work.

In fact, the prince was not endorsing rebelliousness. He just wanted to look like everybody else: like every high-school teacher, like every middle manager with a sport-utility vehicle, like every off-duty police officer. The prince made a brave leap into conformity – which is precisely why the American media were so proud of him.

I remember a TV ad from that year: it was selling an SUV, and showed office workers bravely discarding their ties as they headed to the freedom of the weekend and the outdoors. The background music ("I don't wanna work/I just wanna bang on de drum all day . . .") was cruise-line calypso – the perfectly non-threatening connoter of utter blandness. If Prince Claus's defiance is already the stuff of boomer-targeted automobile ads, you know that it is the most cautious stance of all.

The casualization of men's clothing is another phase in the worldwide sprawl of the suburban mega-chains – the Gap, J. Crew, Eddie Bauer, Roots – and by those vast empires of bland, Polo, Nike. . . . This is the global hegemony of the mall, the aesthetic that systematically stamps out signs of sensitivity or sensuality in men.

Ties are subversive in such a culture, for they are the most sensual aspect of the business uniform. They are the banker's one channel of self-expression, of poetry. The lush triangle of tie in an executive's charcoal facade is the one window onto his soul. The suits may be matte wool, manly dull, but the tie is delicate silk, an impractical substance: it is the kind of thing women's clothes are made of.

Actually, generalized casualization is not inevitable or inexorable. Indeed, I believe it is out of

grounds, you are a poseur and a fraud.

Of course, this consideration has never bothered Americans much, and so the image of the loud American blithely walking into an English gentlemen's club, wearing a tie proclaiming his service in some ancient, elite military unit – the Household Cavalry or the Life Guards or somesuch – thus provoking offence and embarrassment, are legendary.

Probably the most famous description of such a faux pas is not by a snobbish Brit but by a laconic American. It comes in Hemingway's *A Moveable Feast*, when the young writer runs into F. Scott Fitzgerald in the Dingo Bar in Montparnasse and notices that his friend is wearing the blue-and-red striped tie of the Life Guards (a tie that was popular at the time because the Prince of Wales wore one). Hemingway writes, "I thought I ought to tell him about the tie, because they did have British ☞

in Paris and one might come into the Dingo – there were two there at the time – but I thought the hell with it and I looked at him some more. It turned out later that he bought the tie in Rome."

These days, unless you are actually spending a lot of time in England with the kind of person who is likely to recognize famous regimental or sporting ties – of whom there are actually very few – you don't need to worry about avoiding certain colours or patterns. Besides, most of the famous ones are so gaudy and ugly that you will not be tempted to buy one in the first place. ✍

fashion. Casual Fridays seem to be dying out; young men are returning to formality. This is partly a reaction, believe it or not, against their fathers: they have seen the old man wearing nothing but khakis and polo shirts to work for the past ten years, and they are rebelling by buying cufflinks and pocket squares. Ties are definitely back.

Nor is the tie uncomfortable. The tie-bashers who complain of tightness are being throttled by their shirt collars, which they should buy larger: the tie has nothing to do with it.

It is true that the tie is a dangerous accessory for those with bad taste. The mere existence of ties sporting jokey cartoon characters, or splatter-painted jungle-prints, worn with green double-breasted suits, is enough, I admit, to turn one off neckwear forever.

It is indeed difficult to know how bold is too bold when it comes to ties; the choosing of pattern and colour is something that most men find stressful, and if you are one of them, then ask someone you like, and trust, for advice. (It's also a good excuse for a joint shopping trip, which is always an adventure in flirting.) But before we get to colours, let us consider how modern ties are made.

Quality

Silk ties used to be cut in the same direction as the weave of the fabric, but knotting them left deep creases, and they wore out quickly. According to Alan Flusser, a tailor who has written a series of useful guidebooks on men's clothes, a New York tailor called Jesse Langsdorf patented an innovation, in the 1920s, whereby he cut the cloth on a forty-five-degree angle to the weave. This is called a **bias** cut. He also patented his method of sewing three pieces of fabric together to create the tie. This design remains the basic pattern.

In a quality tie, the vertical seam on the underside will be hand-sewn. This is quite rare, so don't worry about it: even very expensive ties are mostly machine-sewn today. You will, however, want to look for a loose stitch closing the seam on the back of the wide end. This may look a little unfinished – indeed all the stitches at either end of the tie may look troublingly loose. It is actually a good sign: the tie cannot be sewn too tightly together or it will lack give: it must be able to be twisted and knotted and crumpled and return to its original shape. In fact, it is the **interlining**, an invisible, spongy cotton or wool-blend stiffener running the length of the tie that gives it its shape, not the stitching.

Interlinings are slightly thicker now than they were twenty years ago, due to the popularity of wider knots. They should be completely covered by the lining. The lining that you see underneath the ends of the tie is not usually of the same fabric or colour as the front of the tie. Expensive ties, particularly from Italy, will sometimes be **self-tipped**; that is, both tips will be lined with the fabric of the tie itself.

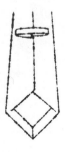

Self-tipped ties are more expensive

The Hermès mystique

I don't really get it, myself. People get all starry-eyed about Hermès ties, say they're the best in the world. Perhaps what they mean is that they have the most convincing marketing. Hermès is a company that has been around for a very long time; since 1837, in fact, when the French manufacturer began making saddles and other leather objects, literally for the carriage trade. Why they then turned their attention to silk scarves and ties I don't know, but they managed to transfer some of the horsey cachet of the saddles to their whimsical but conservative apparel. The ties are, to many men, particularly Europeans, the epitome of masculinity. They are certainly well-made: very thick and heavy, they make knots the size of baseballs, knots worthy of Big Men. The patterns on them are small and busy: they are ☞

Expensive tie-makers also like to advertise the fact that the **loop,** the little circle of fabric sewn onto the back, supposedly to hold the thin end in place, is made of the same silk as the rest of the tie, and has both its ends sewn firmly inside the seam. As with all such useless details, it is an indication of a great deal of labour, but says little about the quality of the silk or the prettiness of its pattern. Besides, most men don't even use the loop.

If you are looking for really absurd luxury, you can find something called a **seven-fold** tie. It is made entirely of one piece of silk, with no interlining. The fabric begins as a square and is folded seven times into the shape of a tie. This gives it its stiffness, without need of invisible canvas. It may or may not look any better than an ordinary tie, but it will certainly cost twice as much.

And of course, as with any item of clothing, if you are truly concerned with quality, and have already endowed your university library and funded a relief effort, you can have a tie custom-made. You can go, for example, to Charvet, in the Place Vendôme (where you can drop in for a twenty-five-dollar cocktail at the Ritz as well), or to Marinella of Naples, a tiny shop in the Piazza Vittoria, where François Mitterrand, Mikhail Gorbachev, King Juan Carlos of Spain, and Bill Clinton have had ties made. This option is useful if you are unusually tall or short, or if you want to tie a special knot which uses a lot of fabric and therefore requires a thinner interlining or a greater length. Or if you just want to show off.

Actually, the best way to judge the quality of a tie is simply to feel it and look at it. If it seems beautiful, it is. If you want a heavy, ribbed silk, which will make a full knot, then go for it. If you prefer a finer weave with a smoother texture, do not hesitate. The most important thing about a tie is not its construction, but its colour.

Colours

The pattern in a tie is generated in two ways: by weaving and by printing. It can come from one or the other or both. For a **woven** pattern, the manufacturer takes yarns already dyed different colours and weaves them together. A **print** is a fabric that is first woven and then dyed (usually by silkscreen). Ties whose pattern comes from weaving tend to have a varied texture as well; increasingly, ties have a pattern in the weave and a different one in the colour – textures are big these days.

The most common woven patterns in ties have been, since around 1900, small and regular squares, diamonds, and checks. These subtle patterns constitute what has become known as a **Macclesfield** tie, after a town in Lancashire, in the north of England, where Chinese and Indian silk was woven. They were especially popular in the 1920s, in shades of grey, black, and white. Because a Macclesfield print is often silvery, it is thought of as a "wedding"

famous for images of interlocking rings and chains, and also for cutesy animals like ducks and dogs. Their conservatism is strangely unsensual to me. I suspect that men collect their thousands of patterns because the brand is so powerful: if you buy something with an Hermès logo on it, you are buying into a history of luxury and privilege, and perhaps you think you are becoming a part of that legend. I don't. Hermès ties make me think of airport duty-free shops, which are not the sexiest of places. ✒

tie – it goes with dark suits, morning coats, and formal wear.

Another English town, **Spitalsfield**, gave its name to a kind of woven silk for ties, in patterns that were slightly larger than the Macclesfield, and more colourful, often combining three or four colours. Most of the woven geometric patterns in high-end stores today would probably be considered Spitalsfields by old-school purists, but the term is now obsolete.

Stripes, usually diagonal, have been extremely popular for the past few years, and the Advanced Class will have fun matching them with striped shirts and suits, as long as all the stripes are of noticeably different sizes and intensities.

Solid colours are extremely useful and elegant. If there is no pattern on your tie, you needn't ever agonize over matching it with a checked shirt and striped suit and floral pocket square. The boldness of the solid tie is also always useful: it projects confidence. Its simplicity is chic.

> "The BOLDNESS of the SOLID tie is USEFUL: it projects CONFIDENCE. Its simplicity is CHIC."

Matching

This is the toughest part of dressing for most men. The delicate art of putting colours together is considered a feminine one, or a gay one, like painting rooms and choosing furniture upholstery. You may or may not be a straight man, but you *are* a man, not a little boy, and you must dress yourself.

The usual male solution is to revert to the tried,

tested, and dull: a blue suit, white shirt, and red tie. This is what politicians wear in order to appear sensible, trustworthy, and ordinary.

It is interesting that the French word *sensible* doesn't mean sensible, it means sensitive – which is a word with a very different, indeed almost opposite meaning, in English. The politicians who want to appear sensible most definitely do not want to appear sensitive; sensitivity is not a reliable characteristic in a military leader. Needless to say, I am going to encourage you to be more sensitive than sensible. For this reason, readers of this book are forbidden to wear a white shirt, red tie, and blue suit, unless you want to be mistaken for a conservative candidate for the Senate, or a midwestern congressman.

Ensure that your tie has a dimple

The other popular option for the cautious man is simply to ensure that all his clothes are differing shades of the same colour. If your suit is blue, then a blue shirt and blue tie are certainly risk-free, but it is also a little unimaginative. It is not actually wrong to colour-match – indeed, bright pink on pale pink could be a daring stroke worthy of the Advanced Class. But generally you should try to match *different* colours in a way that seems, to your own entirely subjective taste, harmonious.

Here are some interesting colour matches to play with. (You will pick and choose among these, of course, according to what works best with your own skin tone, eye colour, and hair.) Try:

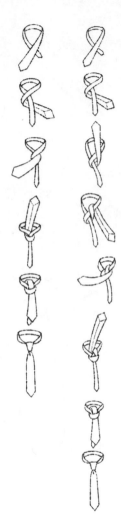

pink shirt/solid silver tie/navy suit/darker pink pocket square

light blue shirt/striped dark rose tie/charcoal suit/steel grey
pocket square

dark (French) blue shirt/solid purple tie/charcoal suit/pat-
terned purple square

white shirt/solid orange tie/navy suit/white linen square

grey striped shirt/solid orange tie/charcoal pinstripe suit/
light blue pocket square

white-and-blue check shirt/brown check tie/mid-grey suit/
dark blue patterned square

Knots

The simplest knot is the one you were probably
taught to tie as a child: it is the four-in-hand.

The four-in-hand makes the most reliably uniform knot; it is also the narrowest. It is still, despite
what many earnest guidebooks will tell you, appropriate for all but the most severely cut-away collars,
particularly with the thick, textured woven silk ties
which are in vogue.

If the four-in-hand makes a knot which is too
small for the collar – that is, if the top corners of the
triangular knot are not covered by the collar points
– tie a half Windsor, which has an extra wraparound.

The full Windsor, which has another extra wrap,
makes a very wide knot which may overwhelm the
face, particularly on smaller men.

There are several other knots with interesting
names. If you are truly interested in these variations,
you can find websites devoted to their dissection, on

Four-in-hand knot (left)
Half Windsor knot (right)

which obsessives will argue about nomenclature and technique. But you don't need to be this nerdy. The basics above will serve any shirt.

Whatever your choice of knot, ensure that the front of the tie has at least one dimple – a depression or half-fold – in it as it emerges from the knot. You create the dimple simply by massaging it, using whatever fingers you have and in whatever way works, as you tighten the knot. A tight knot almost always ensures a dimple. A smooth, convex tie-front is unsensual; a dimpled or ruffled tie is more textured and expressive. The Advanced Class, and those with plenty of fingers, can experiment with double dimples for a ruffled effect – a desirable dandyism.

The Bow Tie

This knot is the one that is most difficult to illustrate using a diagram, because the crucial action is a sort of stuffing motion which happens behind the front of the tie. So I will give you a verbal step-by-step along with the diagram on the next page. Practise this first around your bare neck without a collar; it's easier.

Here we go: Make the right end (we'll call it end A) about five centimetres longer than the left end (B). Cross A over B, bring A under and through. Hold A up, the end near your nose, while you fold B and move it to a horizontal position, under A. The front of the bow is now in place. Drop A down vertically over B. Now the only tough part: you are going to bring A under and behind the knot you have

Full Windsor knot

How to tie a bow tie

just formed, while simultaneously folding it in two. The fold will come exactly where the right edge of the back layer of the finished bow will be. Stuff it through the knot just behind the front layer of the bow. Pull it out the other side. Flatten, straighten, adjust by pulling on the folded ends. Don't worry if you can't get it perfectly symmetrical: a wonky bow tie is the sign that it is self-tied.

Most men will only ever wear a bow tie with formal dress, which is why you might want to practise this before you are late for your party and your companion is telling you that the taxi is outside and you are sweating and swearing in front of the mirror. But this also provides an occasion to discuss the infamous bow tie in general – as an option for day, with a suit or sports jacket. The subject of bow ties creates an emotional response. The class-conscious man recoils at the idea that anyone could sell, let alone wear, a pre-tied or "made-up" bow tie. On the other hand, left-wingers recoil at what they perceive to be a symbol of political conservatism. And followers of fashion wrinkle their noses at the anachronism. The bow tie is one of those deliberate eccentricities which basically dull men employ in an attempt to be zany and fun.

In fact, anachronism is often the point. The bow-tie wearer is a man who openly disdains changing fashions. He uses his tie as a symbol of connection to the past, as one might wear spats or a fob watch. He is not necessarily an economic conservative, but he is a social conservative. He is the kind of man who writes thank-you notes and calls people Mister until invited to do otherwise. If this sounds rather proper, it's deliberate: the bow tie is the embodiment of propriety.

Which explains its long connection with the newspaper business. The newspaper or magazine editor deals with words, an arcane medium. His bow tie is a badge of fastidiousness – a quality of the greatest importance when dealing with words. The fussier we are about language, the more precise we will be.

Some guidelines: butterfly-shaped ties are called **thistles**; the straight ones with pointed ends are called **bat's wing**. The ends of thistles should not exceed six centimetres in width; bat's wings are usually narrower. (These widths, of course, will change over the decades with fashion.) The bow itself, as it lies across your collar, should never be wider than your face or extend beyond the outer edges of your collar, or it will dwarf your ensemble.

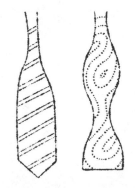

Bat's wing (left) and thistle bow ties

Be aware that a patterned bow tie for daytime wear automatically marks you as proud and a little odd. Paul Fussell, in his book on social class in America, says that bows are shunned by the genuine upper classer, but the British *Sloane Ranger Handbook* illustrates them as acceptable old-boy accoutrements. To me, they signal someone with a huge brain but not an overwhelming Latin sensuality. In other words, it is not the mark of a ladies' man. The word *dapper* comes to mind – not a sexy word, indeed a word with a connotation of smallness.

But it all depends how you do it. Martin Amis, in *The Information*, describes an author playing billiards, wearing "a charcoal three-piece suit of tubular severity, plus rigid bow tie." Now "tubular severity" could be actually sexy. Bear it in mind for your dinner jacket.

Ascots and Scarves

The Royal Ascot races take place every June in Ascot, Berkshire, and have been since 1711. Ascot provides the best annual opportunity for the British upper classes to bring out their **morning coats**, which is the correct dress for the Royal Enclosure. The ensemble, also worn to daytime weddings, consists of grey pinstriped trousers, a grey or charcoal cutaway frock coat, a dove grey or buff waistcoat, a plain shirt with plain turndown collar, a tie of any colour (yes), and a grey or black top hat.

Now, the tie is where it gets interesting: it is also permissible to wear, with morning dress, a rather more spreading, more simply knotted cravat, usually silver, often stuck with a pearl-topped pin. This fulminant expression of silk is what became known, some time in the middle of the nineteenth century, as the **ascot** – which has now come to mean the simple neckscarf we associate with playboys of the 1960s, with David Niven in a blue blazer or Hugh Hefner in a silk dressing gown. It is a wide-ended silk tie that is loosely knotted and goes inside an open collar. It has been considered old-fashioned; you pretty much see it only on not-quite-U country-club types with Jaguars and little leather moccasins for driving. (The British still call ascots cravats.)

That is, until now – for, believe it or not, it's coming back. Loose scarves and cravats of all kinds, for a more casual and less prim look, are appearing in fashion spreads and store windows. And the ascot itself is surfacing among the campier fashion-forward set. At this point in its revival the line between the ironic and the earnest is disappearing; the ascot's slide into serious dressing is almost complete. And it looks pretty cool on a younger guy.

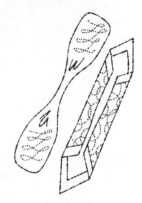

Ascot tie (left) and neckerchief

I myself prefer the neckerchief to the ascot. It creates, under an open collar, a workmanlike, sort-of Errol Flynn ruggedness, as if you have been working in the hot sun. But you don't use a cotton bandana like a true workman, no: you use a printed silk foulard and express your sensitivity and refinement at the same time. You just take a large square silk scarf – not an ascot, which is narrowed in the part that goes around your neck – and fold over two corners so it becomes a rectangle. Then you narrow it one more time. Then you just knot it once and tuck the ends inside the shirt. Try it with a tweed jacket. The delicacy and expressiveness of the silk makes a nice contrast with the conservative manly roughness of wool.

Of course, if you can take yourself seriously as Cary Grant or Fred Astaire or Sean Connery circa 1960, try the ascot.

The Pocket Square

In a 1939 British novel called *Party Going* – O enticing title! – there is a mysterious character called Embassy Richard. At least, the other characters call him that, because of his habit of attending all the chic embassy parties in London. How does he do it? He simply crashes. He dresses in his impeccable evening wear and strides in and graciously accepts a drink. The point is, if you're confident enough, no one will challenge you.

Cut to Canada in about 1990, and my father dressing for a black-tie event in the same narrow dinner jacket he has had since he was eighteen or twelve or something. He calls me in, agitated: he is about to attempt something momentous. He is showing a centimetre of straight white linen in his breast pocket. "What do you think?" he asks, breathless, appalled by the enormity of his own daring, like a man preparing to heave a hand grenade at an archduke. "Is it too . . . *Embassy Richard*?"

And here is the crux of the pocket-square problem: Embassy Richard is elegant, but he is also slightly ridiculous (at least to the kind of WASP male who has been wearing the same dinner jacket since he was four). The edge of linen connotes, to my father, a 1950s glamour, a Cary Grant chic, but it

verges on the oily, on Rick's Café Américain territory: too much of the pocket square and the signet
ring and you might as well be wearing cologne and
smoking a hookah.

Which makes it even more fascinating that the
floppy dash of colour and shine in the gentleman's
breast pocket has made a huge comeback in North
America in the last twenty years. Again, this is part
of a return to formality. The continent is growing
up: the dressy male is no longer an object of fear
and derision. Men, even young men, are feeling
less constrained in their sartorial flourishes, embrac-
ing cufflinks, pocket squares, and even cologne.
Who hasn't had a fantasy of coming off like an
Italian cabinet minister, or at the very least a
Parisian barrister?

The square gives you the opportunity to experiment with the current vogue for a profusion of
texture: there is nothing more sophisticated than a
guy who has managed to match a solid shirt, checked
tie, striped suit, and paisley pocket square. Women
instinctively know that such a man must be good in
bed, because he is obviously a sensualist.

There are, of course, certain suits – particularly
very hip, fashion-forward suits, with body-hugging
lines – which would be spoiled by such a conservative touch. Cotton suits worn with polo shirts and
Chelsea boots, or shiny black suits worn with rayon
sports shirts, do not cry out for embellishment. But
I myself rarely wear a suit without a puff of some

"The FLOPPY dash of COLOUR and shine in the GENTLEMAN'S breast POCKET has made a huge COMEBACK in North America in the LAST twenty years."

How to fold a pocket square

kind. I even enjoy breaking the convention that says that you shouldn't wear a pocket square unless you are wearing a tie. Why not? I love going out in tweed, jeans, and an open-neck shirt, with a delicate silk square softening the rough nubble of my jacket. I think it looks debonair.

The adjoining diagrams are for those in search of Old World elegance.

The pointy look is only possible with linen, or with starched fine cotton; it's very formal, very fifties, and is perhaps best saved for black tie.

It is important to note, however, that the advice that guidebooks and salesmen give you (only silk pocket squares should be displayed tousled and puffed; only linen ones should be pressed and folded into points, etc.) varies widely. One guy says that you never show the edge of a silk puff, another says you always do; one guy says never neatly fold a silk one, another shows it beautifully done. Obviously, with so much disagreement among experts, it is clear that these so-called conventions are not well established.

Conclusion: Don't listen to anybody.

Pocket squares, with ties, are an expression of sensuality and caprice in an otherwise sober and uniform facade. Puff them, tweak them, fold them to best suit your unique character. If the square has a pretty border – and neatly finished edges – by all means let your breast pocket sprout floppy corners. Or not. If you want the crisp (and, unfortunately, rather finicky and prudish) impression that pressed linen gives, show off as many sharp angles as you want. Or stuff it in like a dishrag. Experiment. This is your four square inches of whimsy.

My own taste is this: the easiest way to puff your square is simply to jam it in in any which way, and leave it. To be *négligé* is to be genteel.

You can also be bold and experimental in how you match your tie and square: aim for complementary but not identical colours, and try to contrast the patterns and textures (paisley square with striped tie; smooth square with textured tie). If you are wearing a coloured shirt, try matching the square to the shirt and not the tie – again, following the pattern versus solid principle.

Finally and most importantly: the pocket square does not replace the plain cotton hanky you should always have hidden in your trouser pocket, for sneezes and tears and for a better grip on a champagne cork when your fingers are slippery with oyster juice. You can buy these in quantity for cheap, and it doesn't matter where. For all I know, Embassy Richard gets his at Wal-Mart. I do know he carries one.

"The POCKET square does NOT replace the plain cotton HANKY you should ALWAYS have HIDDEN in your TROUSER pocket."

CHAPTER SIX

HARDWARE

To call a fashion wearable is the kiss of death. No new fashion worth its salt is ever wearable.

— EUGENIA SHEPPARD

Aaron, a high priest who makes his appearance in Exodus, was instructed by Moses – and this order came down all the way from head office – to sport a breastplate made of engraved gold, held together with gold chains and encrusted with rubies, topaz, emeralds, sapphires, diamonds, and seven other gems. Which is fine if you're a high priest. But until you receive similar instructions from Moses, you may want to go easy on the gold chains and rubies. Or risk appearing rather flash.

Not that the contemporary high priests of commerce don't still like to proclaim their status with gold, even in the middle-class business uniform. Men who have achieved success often feel that the

dark cloth and cotton shirt don't adequately convey
that status. After all, the twenty-eight-year-old
junior partner wears exactly the same uniform; there
are no official rank badges. So the vainglorious man
adds a watch with an expensive name (and it is essential that the name be recognized); a gold bar to close
a collar (that is already buttoned); a gold bar to keep
tie close to shirt (in case tie gets caught in non-
existent machinery); rings; chunky cufflinks.

Now, some of these accoutrements – cufflinks in
particular – can add a subtly expressive element to
an otherwise sober facade. But if you wear all of
them at once you will look more like a mobster than
a powerful ecclesiast.

How to sort through them?

The **collar bar** pins the underside of the collar,
running under the tie's knot. Some run through
two holes in the collar (you must have a collar with
two eyelet holes already sewn in), exposing two
little gold balls – or, worse, jewels – on either side.
The bar's ostensible purpose is to lift and project
the tie knot (its true purpose, as with all of these
faux functions, is merely to project raw pecuniary
worth). To me, a piece of jewellery interfering with
the collar looks about as elegant as a silver tooth in
a wide smile: brash and unsubtle. Ditto for **tie bars**
and **chains,** the things that clip onto a button on the
shirt front (usually the fourth one down) and mar
the front of your tie with a band or chain of gold.

"MEN who have achieved SUCCESS often feel that the DARK cloth and COTTON shirt don't ADEQUATELY convey that STATUS."

Again, the ostensible purpose is to hold your tie against your shirt; the true purpose is to draw attention to a gaudy bauble.

The **watch chain**, on the other hand, I must admit, rather amuses me, largely because of the charmingly clumsy antique watch it implies. Any man daring enough to forgo a wristwatch, wear a waistcoat (for it requires a waistcoat), and carry a pocket watch is the sort of maverick dandy I admire. The chain must be attached to the second-lowest button of the waistcoat (the lowest button being always, of course, undone), with the watch hiding in an outer waistcoat pocket (called a **fob** pocket). Note that the word *fob* is confusing: it can refer to the pocket or the chain or to a leather tab attached to the end of the chain.

Cufflinks I also adore, because the wearing of French cuffs is one of my greatest pleasures. This is traditionally an area where male whimsy has been tolerated, and so you can find humorous cufflinks and symbolic cufflinks – little watering cans, little tennis rackets, footballs, hot and cold taps, whatever – at the most conservative of men's stores. It seems the more cigar-scented the store, the goofier the doodads. This sort of thing is fun if small and not immediately noticeable, garish if large.

Indeed, the same can be said of all cufflinks: skip the enormous square onyx blocks. Gemstones should be reserved for black tie. Gold ovals or rectangles may be engraved with your initials (mine bear my great-grandfather's). And ones with **chain**

"Torpedo" style, chain-linked, and fabric-knot cufflinks

links, as opposed to the push-through or "torpedo" variety, are generally more expensive and desirable, as both faces – one on either side of the cuff – are presentable.

The simple **fabric knot** link – available in bright and sober colours for about twelve dollars everywhere – is artistic and more casual, still preferable to a plain button.

But wear them – or any of these shiny highlights – because they match your outfit, not as a badge of wealth. Your mere presence, if it is elegant and contained, will proclaim your power. Badges? We don't need no stinking badges.

Watches

In recent years, several of the world's most famous watchmakers have launched spectacularly expensive advertising campaigns in an effort to imbue their scientific and technical watches with the glamour of war and adventure, thereby providing the closest contact to war or adventure most men will ever have. Omega paid untold thousands to a Hollywood studio to ensure that Jamesbondman Pierce Brosnan was wearing their Seamaster Professional Divers watch in *Tomorrow Never Dies*. (In the film, Bond uses the watch's *built-in laser* to cut through the armour plating of a speeding train, thus escaping *certain death*!) Omega also made available to the public the X-33, the only watch to have been worn on the moon, which gives you both Mission Time

Matching

Those who are extremely sensitive to aesthetics will notice if your cufflinks are gold and your watch is silver, or if your belt buckle is silver and your cufflinks gold. They will say that the metals clash. I myself am an extremely sensitive guy and I confess that I rarely notice these things. Perhaps I am instinctively sympathetic to those who cannot afford a series of watches to match different outfits. It is true that belts should match, more or less, one's shoes: that is, brown shoes demand a belt which is brownish, but not necessarily of exactly the same shade. Black shoes require a black belt. Gold shirt studs should only be paired with gold links; ditto for silver. But do you need to worry if your gold cufflinks don't match your dull pewter belt buckle? Well, it would be better if they did, but it's not worth stressing about: Most people will notice the cuffs and not the belt. ❧

and Universal Time, whatever that means. Swiss rival Breitling surpassed even Omega in absurdly useless gadgetry: their B-One aviation watch stuffs the face both with hands *and* a digital display, including two time zones, a slide rule for quick calculations, and backlighting that is "compatible with night-vision goggles."

I remember receiving almost aggressive invitations from the publicity machine of the Swiss über-technicians TAG Heuer, who wanted me to attend "interactive" press conferences in a luxurious restaurant. I'm very glad I didn't go: they lectured trapped fashion reporters about the car-racing, fighter-piloting history of their number-crammed timepieces, insisting on the crucial distinction between a "chronometer" (which means a very accurate watch) and a "chronograph" (which means a very accurate stopwatch). For just a few thousand dollars more than the watch you are now wearing, you can have one that gives you a 1/10th of a second display – you'll never miss the 6:15 to Parkingville again!

All these watches look the same, which is to say very ugly. They are festooned with knobs and dials and hands and rotating bezels. (The bezel is the outer ring with numbers on it – it works as a timer, and I'm not sure all the CEOs use it regularly.) All this publicity, of course, is not aimed at yachtsmen and commandos; it's aimed at you and me, people who just need to know – to within five minutes or

Choose the one on the left

so – whether it's lunchtime yet. The point is not to

help you find your bearings in space, but to add to your business suit the invincible manliness and glamour of an astronaut. (Which reminds me of the math professor at my university who walked around with a tool kit on his waist, in case he was ever stuck in an elevator and needed to repair it. He didn't exude glamour. All he exuded was weirdness.)

Victorian gentlemen hid their watches in their pockets, because a true gentleman didn't concern himself with the passing of time. The same is true today. The higher you are on the social ladder, the farther away you are from the actual running of machinery. The train driver may need a stopwatch, but you, sitting in the lounge car reading Proust, don't even need a second hand. TAG Heuer's marketing of the word *chronometer* is typical of their more-is-better aesthetic, and emblematic of its pretentiousness – for a gentleman would never use four syllables where he could use one.

The most elegant watches, the ones that connote education rather than mere riches, are the simplest and plainest. London's upper-middle class, known as Sloane Rangers, wear "old, plain and gold" timepieces – battered childhood watches are fine; even a Rolex is too flash. The French social equivalent, the "BCBG" elite, allow themselves old gold Cartiers or else very cheap Swatches.

Here's the other big secret of watch style: you don't need an expensive one. Almost all of them have quartz function now, which is just as accurate

Key-chain chic

Keys in your pocket are problematic. There is nothing better at giving an impression of awkwardness, of flusteredness, than the metallic racket of a pocketful of coins, keys, penknives, that signals your approach from ten feet away. The only thing you can do to muffle this fanfare is to reduce the power-mania that drives you to carry every house, office, car, garage, boat, and snowblower key that you own. I know it makes you feel in control, like the superintendent who can open every secret door in the building, but there are more elegant ways of projecting power (charcoal pinstripe suits, for example). If you absolutely must have more than four or five keys on your person at all times, carry them in your briefcase.

An interesting alternative adopted by the non-suit-wearing is to display your keys proudly on your belt. You see this among tough guys in jeans ☞

and cowboy boots, and among baggy-pants skatepunks. The cowboy-boot guy favours a simple D-ring clipped to the belt loop, leaving the keys hanging over the front pocket. This is a handyman effect one might classify as Janitor Chic; it connotes ownership of a fleet of large machines.

The trend toward ornamental key chains in the rave-skate-snowboarder milieu is more complex and interesting. Here, the keys are not on display, but the long key chain or wallet-chain is a necessary accessory. The keys themselves are invisible in the pocket. A few years ago, the mode was for bright plastic chains with large links (a nod to the bright artificiality of much of techno culture, as seen in plastic hair barrettes and shiny synthetic knapsacks). Then the plastic links gave way to wooden beads – large, round, and multi-hued, looking something like swollen rosaries.

Interestingly, the long, ornamental key chain ☞

in every watch – accurate enough for those who aren't timing Olympic swimming events, anyway. So all you're paying for is style. Outwardly, a fifty-dollar Timex looks very similar to a five-thousand-dollar Cartier. You can find the plainest Timex with a plain white face, a round gold rim, and a black leather strap. Sure, the Cartier is a little thinner, and the Roman numerals are a little more elegant. But are they $4,950 more elegant?

If you honestly have nothing better to do with five grand – and, again, that means you've thought of all the paintings you could buy, all the short films you could fund – at least buy a slim Cartier Vendôme and not a chunky Rolex. (In the same league, the Piaget "Tradition" is also nice and refined, as is the Hermès "Arceau.") Whatever you buy, stick to plain leather straps; metal straps are literally flashy and give that fatal connotation of machinery.

Digital watches, needless to say, are unacceptable for any outfit or situation except actual triathlon competition. And avoid all secondary dials, numbers, and helium decompression valves. The true James Bond, despite what Omega's marketers attempt to force on him, would not mar his dinner jacket with machinery.

Manly Gifts

There are several masculine accoutrements which are luxuries most men won't buy for themselves: and so they make excellent Christmas and birthday gifts. Here are some suggestions for extra hardware for the man who has everything:

Uselessly expensive shaving gear.

A real badger-hair brush is supposed to absorb more lather and be easier on the skin. Whether the difference it makes is worth a thousand dollars (for the top-of-the-line American badger's back hair) is an irrelevant question. We are after absurdity here. The next step down is boar bristles, and they're actually quite affordable: consider a sleekly modern aluminum brush with a matching razor – they should sell for around one hundred dollars together.

The gentleman's flask.

Plain pewter ones or chrome ones sell for under a hundred dollars. Silver ones cost more, but are less practical as they need to be polished. These are actually extremely useful for discreet nips during sporting events, sermons, and literary readings. A drop of brandy does wonders for bus-terminal coffee. He will use it once a year, but even sitting on a shelf it is a comforting symbol of the past, of a perhaps mythical image of an Edwardian gentleman in a tweed suit. You can also have it soberly engraved with his initials, providing another symbolic link to his great-grandfather, who would also have done such things.

A leather-bound address book,

small enough to fit in a suit pocket. The problem with electronic

echoes another, previous subculture's ornamentation: they look almost identical to the long watch-chains of the zoot-suiter.

The zoot suit was a brief flare in American sartorial history, dating to the early forties, and primarily associated with jazz music. It was named after a pop song of the same name, beboppers being into nonsense rhymes ("later alligator" and "in a while, crocodile" date from the same era). Like skatewear, it was urban and aggressively marginal (often being worn by black and Hispanic musicians). It consisted of extremely high-waisted trousers ("grip hips") with multiple pleats, and an extremely long jacket with huge shoulders ("drape shapes"). It was often worn with an absurdly long watch-chain (a "dog chain") that hung to the knees.

The zoot suit became illegal in the U.S. in 1942 when the American ☞

War Production Board cracked down on the wasteful use of wool. It resurfaced briefly in the early fifties and died. The modern skater's trousers are similarly excessive; a defiant dandyism, like the zoot suit, associated with a musical underground. The chain, in both cases, is purely useless decoration, designed to baffle and irritate the sensible. 〜

organizers is that once an address is erased, it leaves no trace. The old-fashioned pencilled entries retain your entire past in their scrawled phone numbers – all the friends you have lost touch with, all the lovers you are trying to forget. We like history; we want to be aware of it. Besides, an actual notebook is lighter and pleasanter to the touch than a piece of plastic.

A fountain pen. Again, even if he's only going to use it for thank-you notes and cheques, it exists for the mere pleasure of holding. It is heavy; it is filled with dazzling words. And I need not decode the symbolism of staining a virginal white page with the silky fluid that flows so smoothly, so *releasingly* from such a firm and powerful tool. It needn't be a five-hundred-dollar Montblanc, either – the simplest sixty-dollar Waterman is an impeccably smooth writer with a traditional marbled finish. Be sure the nib is fine, however, not the more commonly sold medium (there is a tiny F or M stamped on it), for modern people are not accustomed to wielding a thick nib. Furthermore, modern paper is of such poor quality that a wide swath of ink will bleed and smudge. Enclose some writing paper with the gift: a tablet of heavy, smooth-surfaced drawing paper from an art-supply store is just as good as boxed notepaper.

Brass collar stays, in individual sizes, are a great little stocking stuffer. Most dress shirts come with plastic stays that fall out in the wash or melt under pressing. And most men don't notice. So their collars curl. But a man with brass collar stays is a details man, a guy with everything under control.

CHAPTER SEVEN

FORMAL WEAR

With an evening coat and a white tie, anybody, even a
stockbroker, can gain a reputation for being civilized.
– OSCAR WILDE

Let us first settle the terminology debate: **tuxedo** is not an incorrect term, merely an American one. The class snob is an anglophile, and so prefers to say **dinner jacket**. Dinner jacket and tuxedo are the same thing; one is British, the other Yankee. As usual, Canadians are caught in between, and so use both.

Some modern salesmen are confusing the issue by calling a dinner jacket a dinner suit, attempting to coin a distinction between this and the *white* jacket, for which they reserve the term dinner jacket. This is a totally new and unnecessary revision of labels, especially since white or cream jackets have now vanished from civilized society, other than as kitschy costumes for undergraduates nostalgic for some mythical Era of Swing. (If you absolutely must wallow in the Vegassy fabulousness of a white dinner jacket, at least keep it to the summer.)

It is interesting that the black-tie outfit is to us the summit of formality – indeed, so formal that it is in danger of extinction (particularly with nervous hostesses now marking "black-tie optional" on their invitations, which is no help at all to a diffident guest – for it was once a shockingly *in*formal outfit for evening.

Until the end of the nineteenth century, evening balls and banquets were strictly white-tie affairs. White tie must be accompanied by stiff shirt-front, high collar, and cutaway frock-coat with tails. The 1870s saw the introduction of velvet collars and lapels with evening coats, which evolved into the satin facings we keep today. In the 1880s and 90s, in Europe as in America, evening dress stuck strictly to this uniform, and included a top hat, a carnation in the buttonhole, and often the crowning evidence of aristocratic aspirations: a monocle. The "buttonhole" – meaning not the hole but the flower in it – was such a crucial element of the dignified male facade that the English poet George Selwyn devised a small flat flask to fit under his lapel and nourish his cut flower with water.

It was that famous dandy Prince Albert (later Edward VII) who loosened things up. When entertaining at his country estate at Sandringham, he

"The BLACK-TIE outfit was once a shockingly *IN*FORMAL outfit for EVENING."

opted for what was at the time a wildly casual dinner outfit, a variation on a smoking jacket – short and double-breasted, with dark bow tie, as worn with daytime suits. (The French word for dinner jacket is still *"un smoking."*) Prince Albert's informal look was soon copied in America, particularly in one legendary incident at an exclusive social club in Orange County, New Jersey. The story goes like this. At the club's autumn ball of 1886, a young hipster with the fantastic name of Griswold Lorillard showed up in a mod, short, single-breasted jacket with silk lapels. He had recently returned from Europe, where he had seen the new style. His disrespect for convention so outraged the hostess that he was asked to leave. But his innovation was to change fashion history, for the ball was being held at the Tuxedo Club (so-called for its location, Tuxedo Park). Hence the name still used in America for the same outfit.

Despite Lorillard's heroic feat, black tie was still reserved for entertaining at home, with white tie expected in public, until the 1920s. Again, it was British royalty who changed the rules. Edward VIII (who became the Duke of Windsor on his abdication in 1936) was known as a fashion plate even when he was a mere Prince of Wales. He began wearing short jackets and soft, pleated shirts to formal events, a habit which was widely copied. The casualization of evening wear continues at an accelerating rate; one wonders if the Duke would be dismayed today by what he has wrought.

The upper classes say "dinner jacket"

Black Tie

Here are the conventions of black tie, most of which have been unchanged for the better part of 100 years. (You do have a few options.)

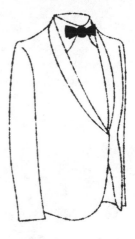

Jacket – black or very dark midnight blue, with **satin** or the coarser-weave **grosgrain** silk lapels. (Grosgrain is a fine silk twill which makes a ribbed weave. The silk with the coarsest ribs is called **ottoman** silk.) Both **single-** and **double-breasted** jackets are acceptable. Both single and double-breasted jackets may have **peak** lapels, which look formal and old-fashioned; **notch** lapels or the rounded **shawl** collar match single-breasted jackets.

Shawl collar

My own personal favourite combination is the single-breasted, one-button jacket with narrow shawl collar in an uninterrupted curve: the Sean Connery/Cary Grant line.

Trousers – black, **uncuffed**, with single black satin ribbon down outside seam. This ribbon is called a **braid**. Your old trousers are probably too wide: get them narrowed all the way down. They may or may not have pleats in front, depending on your taste and your girth. They may be held up with suspenders, or with self-adjusting tabs. **No belt.** The trousers should not even have belt loops.

Shoes – **plain black, lace-up, shiny.** No metal buckles or tasselled loafers. **Patent leather** – the leather with the perfect, unnatural shine – and **court pumps** (slippers with a low vamp and a little bow) are conventionally acceptable. I like the patent leather, but personally I would as soon wear a pink tutu as court pumps.

Cummerbund or waistcoat – you may wear either, but not both. Neither one is necessary. This is another interesting cultural divide: the cummerbund is also an Americanism. Don't believe the guidebooks' warnings about cummerbunds being essential. You don't need one. In Britain, the traditional dinner jacket comprises a waistcoat or an unadorned satin waistband. The waistband on most formal trousers is going to be slightly wider than normal anyway, and quite flashy if it is satin. The British look at it this way: Your jacket is going to be closed the whole time, right? (One would *hope* it is, anyway.) You may open it when sitting down to dine, at which point no one can see your midriff anyway. Try telling this to a determined salesman at Snappy Rentals: he is going to act all outraged and warn you of humiliation if you show your face in public without this ridiculous shiny band at your waist. It is up to you to be firm. Remember that he is trying to sell you things which are going to cost you more money.

Personally, I'm not too big on waistcoats either, which clutter the snow-white shirt-front. Just avoid a belt; suspenders are appropriately invisible.

"You may wear EITHER a CUMMERBUND or WAISTCOAT, but not BOTH."

The matching sets of patterned waistcoats and bow ties that you can also get at Snappy Rentals are to be avoided: they make you look like a small-town pharmacist trying to be original.

Shirts and collars – now it gets complicated. The standard shirt front has narrow pleats, but an elegant variation is the white **piqué**, or "Marcella," front: that waffle-textured pattern (usually worn with white tie). Some shirts have a **fly front**, meaning a strip of fabric covering the buttons, in which case you don't need studs. If the buttonholes are visible, you need **studs**, which must be small and severe: plain black (onyx or jet or even glass), gold, or mother-of-pearl. Regular plastic buttons will not do. You also must have cufflinks.

Regular turndown collars are finally beating the precious wing collar into obsolescence, and I for one am pleased. The wing collar's height pushes against a double chin and makes a full-faced or overweight man look constrained and puffy. Second, the wing collar exposes the metal clasp and slider on the tie, at the back. (Of course, in a less democratic country, one would be able to buy a bow tie without a slider, in one's exact size, but everything here fits all.) And yes, one can now buy some wing collars with a "tunnel" around the collar to hide the bow-tie strap, but I still disapprove.

Do not in any circumstances wear a collarless or tab-collar shirt, particularly with a jewel at the

"Regular TURNDOWN collars are FINALLY beating the precious WING COLLAR into OBSOLESCENCE."

White tie

There are very few places left on earth where white tie is still demanded of gentlemen. These events include certain formal dinners at the White House, Buckingham Palace, and other royal courts of Europe. White tie requires a long, cutaway tailcoat, a wing collar, and a low-cut white waistcoat. If you wear black tie with tails, you are a waiter. It is a faux pas to ostentatiously wear white tie to a black-tie event. Indeed, white tie is becoming extinct even in embassies and palaces. You may wear your medals and other decorations only with white tie, unless your black-tie invitation speci-fies "Decorations." ❧

throat. This is the dreaded Pro Athlete at Awards Ceremony aesthetic.

My own black tie of matte grosgrain silk is exactly 15½ inches long and has no clasp or slider, and was bought at Gieves & Hawkes on Savile Row. It is interesting that this tailor provides formal wear in regulation specifications to the British armed forces, and thus is a kind of textbook of conservatism. The regulation width for a British navy black tie is 2½ inches at the ends, which is surprisingly wide.

The tie, needless to say, must be real, that is to say self-tied and not horrifyingly "made up." Contrary to popular belief, it is easy to tie a bow tie (see the diagram in the previous chapter).

Keep everything – tie, lapels, trouser legs – narrow.

If you are in doubt as to whether black tie is appropriate for an event (as with those ambiguous "black-tie optional" invitations), then do not wear it. You are always safer being underdressed than overdressed.

"Black-Tie Optional"

This brings up the stressful question of the frustrat-ingly vague invitation. What does "optional" mean? Do I dress up or not?

If you see this phrase on an invitation, it means that the following hesitations have taken place: it means that the planners of the party began by envi-sioning a glittering formal affair, with neatly

groomed men in stark black and white as sober back-
drops for the dramatic colour and flashes of flesh of
the women. And so they wrote "Black Tie" on the
invitations – and then immediately had doubts.

This is what has gone through their minds: What
if this seems too snobby? What if we are excluding
those without the resources to own a dinner jacket?
What if we are insulting the men with beards and
Jethro Tull albums who don't believe in such elitist
dress and who may refuse on principle to come to
such a stuffy affair?

*White tie requires a long
cutaway tailcoat*

And so the "Black-Tie optional" cop-out.
Meaning, We hope most of you will be in black tie,
but we won't bar entrance to anyone who isn't.

Now, this should go without saying. What host
is going to send a guest home for failing to live up
to the dress code? It's not 1886. It's the guest's
problem if he feels frumpy and out of place all
night, not the host's.

Note to party planners: this instruction is of no
use to anyone. It throws all invitees into a panic.
What everyone about to step into a crowded public
place wants to know – and has always wanted to
know, since the invention of alcohol itself – is *what
will everyone else be wearing?*

The "optional" clause removes all certainty. It
says to men, who are naturally unsure about clothing anyway, "This party is a kind of quiz: your
response is up to you, pal." Now, you know that
the Jethro Tull brigade – any rock music critics or

Canadian novelists who happen to be invited – will welcome the opportunity to forgo formal dress and gleefully show up in their comfy sweaters. You know that some people will be in dark business suits, some in ruffled shirts and court pumps with little bows. You know that if you are one of three people in a crowd of five hundred who has actually applied a bow tie and stiff shirt ("donned the soup and fish," as P.G. Wodehouse's aristocratic characters call it), you will feel ridiculously shiny and frilly. If you have this feeling – that few guests will actually be wearing black tie – then don't. It is far safer to be understated than over-fancy.

"Every GROWN-UP man should OWN a DINNER JACKET."

In other words, if the host wants black tie, she should say black tie, or she will end up with a motley party. And what of the sensitive men who don't own a dinner jacket and don't think they should, as it would be vaguely decadent, and feel resentful of any effort to make them acquire one? Well, if they are opposed to decadent glamour, then they shouldn't want to attend the party at all.

Every grown-up man should own a dinner jacket, just as he should own a dark suit, and those who do not prize such old-fashioned values may sanctimoniously decline invitations to any fabulous party peopled by handsome men and dazzling women with bare shoulders and cleavage. Take your pick of value systems.

For the grumblers I know – middle-classers to a man – the issue is not financial, either. Before insisting that you can't afford a dinner jacket, tell me the value of your stereo. Then add the value of your TV and your MP-3 player. Then tell me you can't afford a sale-rack tuxedo.

Indeed, one standard black tuxedo (available for a couple of hundred bucks at massive New Year's sales every January at every conservative men's store in every town and village on this continent) is cheaper than three rentals. So it pays for itself in one year. Remember that dinner jackets don't need to be of very high quality: you wear them only a couple of times a year, so they won't wear out. And a black fabric is a black fabric from a few feet away, whether it's wool and polyester or pure cashmere. Vintage stores are also excellent sources, for the basic design of the outfit has not changed in fifty years.

Furthermore, an impecunious gentleman can always wear a dark business suit and tie and be accepted at any formal function.

"Creative" Black Tie

Over the past ten years, fashion designers and high-end men's retailers have been battling to disrupt or render obsolete the conventions of black tie I have just delineated. They have been pushing black shirts and black ties (tied with a regular four-in-hand) for a gothic/fascist sheen, or black suits with white shirts and silver ties for a morning dress/evening dress crossover, or wing collars with four-in-hand knotted ties for an Edwardian-barrister look. These men are not just twenty-five-year-old fashion publicists, either; increasingly, the innovators include men over thirty. The tide has truly turned.

I deplore this trend, but it can only gain ground, as it is being pushed by the most powerful people in the world: the movie stars who want to look original at the Oscar ceremonies. Their formal getups are breathlessly and instantly reported by media around the world, and go on to influence the front-window display at Fit-Rite in your hometown.

"Creative" black tie – velvet smoking jackets, cravats, black shirts, band collars, any variation on the penguin uniform – is a domain only available to the truly confident, the man who is conscious of style and emphatic in his unorthodox choices. He doesn't need my advice on any aesthetic issue and indeed is probably not reading this book. Messing with the conventions of the dinner jacket is for the sartorial Advanced Class, in which successes and failures are equally magnified. A man without impeccable taste who attempts to individualize this uniform (for it is a uniform, and its attractiveness lies precisely in its uniformity) risks looking like a snickering juvenile. There is nothing more pathetic than a failed flamboyant.

I am thinking, here, of all the would-be "defiant" modifications of the proudly casual Boomer generation, such as Woody Allen's canvas sneakers (worn to an awards ceremony). These kitsch accoutrements are supposed to be humorous, because ex-hippies feel guilty about appearing to take style seriously. But when basketball superstar Dennis Rodman, a man who takes style very seriously indeed (definitely Advanced Class), wears a velvet bow tie and velvet top hat to the Oscars, he is not being kitschy or anti-snob: he genuinely loves that hat. He is being more of a style snob than a vaguely socialist rebel.

This is admirable, but it has created an unpleasant fallout. The Dennis Rodmans of the world are creating pressure on salesmen and ordinary consumers to be more original. Paradoxically, this does not entail greater freedom for men; it means greater confusion. It will lead to far more disastrous experiments, and an overall rise in tackiness. When men could rely on uniforms, they could rely on the rules of those uniforms to make them look great. Now you must rely on your own taste (and not on any salesman's). If ever you are in doubt about the tastefulness of any outfit – if you worry that black on black on black makes you look like a mod undertaker, for example – then you will always be safe with the standard black suit, white stiff-front shirt, and bow tie. This is an extremely flattering outfit, and it is nothing to be ashamed of.

It is true that the "creative" option is much cheaper to assemble. Youthful stores with techno music playing will sell you black velvet suits for half the price of a real dinner jacket. A long black frock coat that shines because it has too much polyester in it will look cheap in daylight, but highly

"When MEN could rely on UNIFORMS, they could rely on the RULES of those uniforms to MAKE them look GREAT."

daring at night. It will look even more formal than an extremely costly Zegna suit in, say, grey glen plaid, simply because it is black. Wear it three times and throw it away, and it will still be cheaper than three rentals.

Here are some guidelines for those who would mess with the penguin paradigm. First, stick to a black suit as your foundation. A certain uniformity is still attractive in a group of dressed-up men, and black and white are still the most formal colours. The only area of fruitful experimentation is in the accents: the shirt, the tie, the waistcoat.

A white piqué shirt – the stiff cotton with the faint waffle texture – is an elegant substitute for a pleated shirt, either with bow or straight tie. Black or white silk T-shirts with simple crew necks are also dramatic with a black suit, as long as you are in great shape. Yes, T-shirts. The formality is maintained by the colour scheme – black and white – not by the presence or absence of a tie.

Flashy waistcoats are fun, particularly when they are embroidered with metallic threads, gold or silver. (This is the one outfit which will not be marred by excessive luxury.) But when you match them with a bow tie in exactly the same fabric you will look too cute, as if you bought your whole outfit as a kit. If you are wearing a gaudy waistcoat, stick to black tie.

Metallic ties – particularly silver – are also very formal. A silver tie (a regular tie, tied with four-in-hand or half Windsor) looks particularly dramatic against a black shirt, although there is a touch of the mobster in such contrast. I am not so much in favour of the white silk tie on white shirt, as it looks washed out.

Readers of this book will never be seen in public with a band collar or with a cute little "lariat" tie.

The exception to the black jacket rule is the midnight blue or plum velvet smoking jacket, worn with black trousers, which I count as accent or highlight, like coloured bow ties or pocket squares. But you had really better be prepared to take some raised eyebrows in this, the dandiest of all dandy ensembles.

A final note on invitations. If the words "black-tie optional" on an invitation hit a panic button for most men, the words "creative black tie" are even worse. Who would want to go to a party, unless it's a fancy dress ball, to be judged by his costume? Men should never be instructed to be creative, or many of them simply will not show up. If you really want a creative and fashionable look from your male guests, but do not want rows of penguins, try writing something totally abstract, such as "Dress: Festive." Such an injunction applies both to men and women. It means your guests don't even have to think about black tie, but it gives them licence to be flashy.

Weddings

Priests in the Church of England used to refuse to marry couples after noon. In the twentieth century,

> "READERS of this book will NEVER be seen in PUBLIC with a BAND COLLAR or with a CUTE little "LARIAT" tie."

Morning dress

this deadline was advanced to 3 p.m. and then to six. They are still reluctant to do it in the evening. This is why tradition-fancying Christians tend to marry in the morning and early afternoon, and Jews are free to marry in the evenings (which makes more sense as far as wild parties go).

All this provides sartorial dilemmas. Very fancy weddings require formal dress, and formal dress for men is different in the day and in the evening. The practice of holding weddings in the evening, and asking men to wear black tie, has led to a great deal of confusion. Some men wear black tie to afternoon ceremonies. This is incorrect. Dinner jackets should not be seen before 6 p.m. – though if you are a guest at a daytime wedding and the invitation says black tie, then you have no choice but to grin and bear it. If you are being married in the day, and really want to follow conventional etiquette, you must wear **morning dress** (not, as it is misspelled in a common Freudian slip, "mourning dress").

The correct morning suit has been much abused by those rental chains with the word *snazzy* foremost in their imaginations. Influenced no doubt by the Las Vegas weddings of country music performers, the rental providers prefer costumes to uniforms. They try to outfit men – on what should be the most serious day of their lives – in costumes for circus performers. They offer pearl grey or champagne tailcoats with contrasting lapels and dramatic cutaways, mushrooming ascot ties with stick-pins, proliferations of entwined flowers on the lapels like a portable bed-and-breakfast.

Before I delineate the crucial and non-crucial elements of correct morning dress, let me assure you that it is unnecessary. It is perfectly acceptable and perfectly elegant to get married or attend a daytime wedding in your best dark business suit. The outfit I am about to describe is for the wealthy only. It must be made to measure, as it is unavailable in stores and horrific when rented.

This outfit, should you choose to go formal, must be worn by at least the groom, the best man, the ushers, and both fathers. It consists, primarily, of a single-breasted charcoal coat with full tails and a single vent. This is the most important element: it must be *dark* grey (sometimes called "Oxford grey"), to give you dignity. The skirts are *not* severely cutaway: they come right around the front up near the waist. Add charcoal trousers with black stripes, a dove-grey waistcoat, a plain white shirt with plain turned-down collar, and a plain tie. Knot it with a regular four-in-hand.

It is usually said that the tie must be plain silver or striped black and silver. This is indeed the convention – but this is one convention that those confident mavericks in the Advanced Class can tastefully break. Rent the movie *Four Weddings and a Funeral* just to see the brilliant and subtle pairings of charcoal coats and burgundy ties or multi-coloured waistcoats in morning dress.

"It is PERFECTLY acceptable and perfectly ELEGANT to get MARRIED or attend a DAYTIME wedding in your BEST dark BUSINESS suit."

Skip the amorphous, spreading ascot tie; it is too luxuriant. Skip the pearl tie pin; it is too much. Skip the wing collar; it is a suburbanite's conception of flash. The waistcoat may be single or double-breasted, and may have small lapels or not, but I prefer the plain single with no lapels. The double-breasted waistcoat looks, to my eye, tight and fussy. Keep it spare – unless you are confident enough in your taste to wear an embroidered champagne or dusty pink silk waistcoat (like Hugh Grant in the last wedding of above-mentioned film). Do not wear an exploding spray of baby's breath in your lapel, as if you were some kind of frilled and embaubled children's birthday cake. A single rosebud or carnation is ornament enough for the sober yet sensitive marrying man.

CHAPTER EIGHT

CASUAL

Any man may be in good spirits and
good temper when he's well-dressed.
— CHARLES DICKENS

asual dress is perhaps the contemporary male's weakest point. We have the suit and tie for weddings and funerals, and we have the khaki shorts and kayaking sandals for the mall. In between is a dark, dangerous no man's land, full of pitfalls and booby traps.

Who has not felt stress on hearing that a cocktail party's required dress will be "upscale casual"? What do these words mean? Do you dress up or not? Upscale casual seems to demand creativity or originality, domains in which the Scylla of blandness rivals the Charybdis of affectation.

Unfortunately, this is an area in which you cannot rely on convention; your own personal taste and instincts must be your guides. Furthermore, casual wear is a moving target: it is the only part of the

Casual dress is possibly the contemporary male's weakest point

male wardrobe which actually does respond to seasonal changes in fashion, and so is hard to pin down from one season to the next. You can rely on some general principles, however, and that's what we can discuss here.

Contrasts

A useful principle with casual dressing is to *contrast your top half and your bottom half.* Always match a narrow bottom half with a looser top half, or vice versa. This is particularly useful if you are skinny. A very form-fitting T-shirt plus some narrow jeans may make you look like a wire. Put a more flowing shirt over the tight trousers. Or wear a tight T-shirt with the baggy jeans. Put baggy with baggy and you might look like an oversized kid: the word *swaddling* may come to mind.

The same goes for colours. Black is extremely useful and will always be cool, so you needn't worry about wearing all black clothes to the occasional gallery opening. However, other colours don't work as well when you wear matchy-matchy outfits. An all-blue ensemble, for example, will look a bit childish. You want to match a blue top half with, say, a grey bottom half.

And think about the drawbacks of an all-white ensemble. I know it seems attractive, particularly when the dog days arrive. White linen looks and feels cool, and it conjures 1940s films of elegant spies in Istanbul, of Panama hats and cigars. You think,

"ALWAYS match a NARROW bottom half with a LOOSER top half, or VICE VERSA."

hey, if this loose white linen shirt looks cool, then the addition of loose white linen trousers will look doubly cool, right? I can look dressy and relaxed at the same time, I will look . . . *Mediterranean*. Well, the men who do this successfully are, in fact, Mediterranean. If you are Mediterranean, or you own a restaurant, or if you have just won the Euro Cup, or you just don't shave very much, you may look convincingly macho in this getup. But there is a downside to the all-white ensemble. For one thing, the overall looseness is asexual. Many linen trousers have drawstring waists. Combine this with the flowing shirt, and what you have is jammies. Make it all white, and you have a particularly virginal set of jammies. You are going to look neither Mediterranean nor macho: what you are going to look is sleepy. So: White pants or white shirt, but not both.

The same principle applies to the latest trend in upscale-casual dressing, which marries an extremely dressy top half and an extremely scruffy bottom half. The result is surprisingly debonair. You wear a fine suit jacket or blazer – even something ridiculously stuffy like a charcoal pinstripe – with a fine white shirt. No tie. A silk pocket square. And jeans. You wear the shirt untucked. The final touch is the crucial one: with this you wear hip sneakers – round-toed Pumas, stripy Adidas, skateboardey Etnies. You can even have bright pink or green stripes on your shoes: the more streetwise the better. It sounds ridiculous, and breaks the old rule about pocket squares being ultra-dressy, but the black-jacket-and-jeans has become the night-time uniform of the under-forty urban crowd. It says that you are stylish (and probably monied) but relaxed and hip as well: it says that you are at ease both on Fifth Avenue and in the dim basement clubs where a little loungey house is spun. It is also part of the general trend toward heterogeneous mixing and layering, which puts ties under hoodies under suits.

Waistlines and Tucking

The height, not the width, of your waistline is the new indicator of youth. Only young people – and young women in particular – seem to notice where your belt hangs. If you have never thought about this, or never noticed that someone wears his pants a little high, then you are over thirty-five. And you have probably never realized how uptight and schoolteacherish the high waistline looks to someone who has grown up watching hip-hop videos and skateboarders.

Not that current fashion demands the extremely low-hanging, boxer-exposing trousers of the old-school rap star. Yes, the belly and groin are society's new favourite erogenous zones, and this is happening to both male and female sex symbols. Young girls show off their pubes precisely because they know it's the one area in which women over thirty-five can't compete; a similar principle applies to deejays with their T-shirts inching up and their pants drooping down to show those jutting hipbones and the line of belly hair (the "love trail") that makes teenage girls get all giggly. Go for it if you have the required flat stomach. But to be moderately cool you don't have to show off your underwear, or the base of your stomach, the way young women do. You just buy slightly looser jeans and let them drop a couple of centimetres. The waistband – particularly of casual trousers – should sit on the hips, not around your dead centre. It's just a difference of a few centimetres, crotch to waist, that distinguishes the trousers in Fit-Rite from the trousers in Downtown, Inc. The lower the waistband, the younger you are. (Suits are different. The trousers of most suits – of all but the hippest suits – are designed to sit higher.)

Now there is a paradox in this trend toward the exposed belly, which is that young people also insist on wearing their shirts **untucked**. Nothing separates generations of North American men more than shirt-tucking practices: the Great Tucking Divide is another thing that you will only be aware of if you are under thirty-five. T-shirts, sports shirts, polo shirts, even quite snazzy rayon dress-up shirts will be left dangling on the younger set, even under expensive three-button jackets. Don't do it when you're wearing a tie. (Some conventions are sacred, at least to me.)

So what's the point, you may ask? If your shirt is hanging over your butt, who can tell where the

"Nothing SEPARATES generations of North American MEN more than SHIRT-TUCKING practices."

174 | MEN'S STYLE

waistline is? Ah, but they can. The under-thirties
have very sensitive looseness-detectors. They can
tell instantly, from where your crotch and back
pockets are hanging, whether you are a downtowner
or a nerd.

You, on the other hand, may not care at all what
the under-thirties think, and I admire that. You may
want your appearance to give off values of reliabil-
ity and responsibility rather than modishness or sex
appeal. And this in turn may appeal to the kind of
partner you want. These are not exhortations to
being a slave to fashion: I am only telling you what
your options are. You choose.

Casual Fridays

The "casual Friday" epidemic which plagued the
corporations and businesses of the Western world
in the 1980s and 90s did little to encourage male
style. We can be thankful that the virus seems to
have been contained and eradicated, but damage
has been done. The injunction to be casual seems to
throw many men into a crisis of confidence.

When casual Fridays began in the 1980s, the idea
was to publicize one's donation to a charity. Once
you gave your small donation – a buck or two – you
were given some kind of badge, which permitted
you to show up at work the following Friday without a tie. If you showed up in your casual clothes
but without your badge, you were hectored into
making a donation.

"The 'CASUAL
Friday'
EPIDEMIC
did little to
ENCOURAGE
male style."

The good side of the practice – the charity part – has long disappeared, leaving only the bad hangover: drab bank counters staffed by tellers in sweatshirts and acid-wash jeans. And casual Fridays led in turn to a casualization of business wear on every other day of the week. People discovered that they were doing their jobs just as efficiently in khaki as in navy, that the company hierarchy didn't disintegrate and Western civilization didn't come tumbling down, and began wondering why they couldn't dress like slobs *all* the time. Now, fewer and fewer offices demand a jacket and tie on all their male employees. Some fields – design, computers, media, publishing, and education – have been resolutely tieless since the 1960s.

This massive blandification saddens me. But what saddens me most is the reasoning behind the trend from its very outset. Why was dressing like a slob ever considered to be a *privilege*? The idea that one would want to *pay* for the privilege of relinquishing one's dignity and symbols of authority is utterly backward-thinking. How have North Americans managed to convince themselves that (a) looking elegant, well-groomed, and powerful is some kind of unpleasant societal imposition, and (b) the clothing required for such elegance is uncomfortable? Anyone with any experience of well-tailored menswear will tell you that a century or more of design evolution has solved any practical problems with waistbands and collars, and rendered the fabrics in men's clothes lighter, softer, and less constricting than any equivalent female outfit. The suit, with heavy leather shoes, is just about the most comfortable and practical costume there is.

Furthermore, one commands respect with one's clothes. There has long been a legend that in the early days of broadcasting, BBC radio announcers were made to wear black tie when they read the evening news. Even though radio announcers are invisible to the audience and can wear anything or nothing at all without affecting the quality of the broadcast, the idea was to instill in *them* the right mood, the proper formality for the seriousness of the occasion. The story is apocryphal, but the idea is correct. We behave better when we are better dressed.

And people, rightly or wrongly, will look to a man in a suit as the authority figure in a time of crisis. Note that CEOs and senior partners rarely take note of casual Fridays. They are meeting with important clients just as often on Fridays as on any other day. And perhaps, also, they are the kind of guy who has learned the value of a dignified facade – and maybe that's part of why they're CEOs in the first place. Think about it. Maybe you're allowed to dress casually in your office every day, but that doesn't mean it's a good idea. If you consistently dress casually, you will consistently *not* look like a CEO.

It's funny, too, that permitting variations on the business uniform has not led to a greater variety and colour in sartorial expression, as one might have expected. Despite promises of freedom, it has led to another uniform: the khaki pants/golf shirt/sports jacket/loafers uniform, a uniform just as innocuous as the grey two-button Fit-Rite suit and red tie.

There is, however, a rebellion afoot. As I have been arguing throughout this book, there seems to be a new spirit of dressing, particularly among young men, in the larger cities of this continent. Partly, this is a result of new styles worn by highly influential hip-hop stars, whose idea of "bling" depends less and less on gold jewellery and baggy sports-team outfits, and more and more, as their music becomes representative of mainstream American tastes, and as they figure more and more prominently in glitzy music awards ceremonies, on velvet suits and ties with enormous knots. This is a wonderful influence on contemporary men and contemporary fashion; it fills the gap between the street and the boardroom. It shows, finally, that one can be stylish and flamboyant and well-dressed at the same time.

I realize, however, that it may be difficult to Just Say No to casual Friday if it has become your company policy. I have some solutions to the dilemma this produces. Don't treat Fridays as a day of enforced ugliness, as an excuse for giving up on your appearance. Instead, use Fridays as an opportunity to display your taste and flair in ways that the suit and tie do not permit. Note that even on Friday, you still must wear a jacket. This is the bare minimum of respectability, even if you are tieless. Not any old

My favourite piece of clothing

We all have attachments to some hopelessly unfashionable item that has served us faithfully for years. I have a pair of black leather trousers, which I have been wearing for about fifteen years. They are in the style of Levi's 501s, and are of an exquisite soft leather, which has now stretched and softened to fit me exactly. I have been mocked many times in book reviews, gossip columns, and on-line forums for this attachment. It embarrasses people. I'm not sure why. It has been called "pretentious," whatever that means. I know it dates me: it is a reminder of my formative teenage years as a punk rocker, and then as a New Romantic and a weekend goth. It advertises my fundamental affinity for loud music and inner-city neighbourhoods, which I have been loath to relinquish ☞

jacket: I am not in favour of brown sports jackets with denim shirts and Dockers. My alternative to the khaki-and-denim uniform is this: the casual, fashion-forward suit.

Upscale Casual

The basics of this look I have described in previous chapters: for a suit you need something slightly flashy, perhaps black, perhaps of an unusual fabric, perhaps with unusual detailing (see the chapter on suits). For a shirt you need your basic bartender shirt (see the chapter on shirts). You will wear it untucked.

You may wear jeans with a cool jacket – a black or navy blazer, or a funky one in another colour if it's really cool, made, say, by a Japanese designer.

If you are in the Advanced Class, you may wear, under your jacket, a wool sweater with a hood that hangs over the back of your jacket.

You may wear a dark-coloured golf jacket over your bartender shirt.

Be careful of sweaters on their own. Grown men in sweaters tend to look a little bit unravelled – sweaters do nothing for the drooping shoulders or the swelling paunch; they cling and sag. Turtlenecks are sexless; V-necks look avuncular, even grandfatherly, on anyone over thirty. Plus they tend to keep the aroma of last night's stir-fry on them all day. Sure, they keep you warm, but so do cashmere sports jackets. You will always feel more confident in a jacket – which squares your shoulders and hides your gut.

The Indefatigable T-shirt

You will read, in almost any guide or history of men's fashion, that the T-shirt is the quintessentially American sartorial item, that it is the United States's single most important contribution to current standards of male dress. It is not true. British sailors wore T-shirts for heavy work in the nineteenth century. And in contemporary high fashion, the most successful proponent of the T-shirt since the 1980s has probably been Giorgio Armani – who is emphatically Italian. (Armani, in fact, waxes particularly Italian when he speaks about the T-shirt. "I've always thought of the T-shirt as the Alpha and Omega of the fashion alphabet," he wrote in the introduction to a 1996 coffee-table book called *The White T*. "The creative universe begins with its essentiality, and, whatever path the imagination takes, ends with its purity.")

No matter. Our cultural histories tend to be written by Americans, so even though these facts are grudgingly acknowledged, no one will admit to any wimpy European influence on this now global sartorial staple.

And in fact T-shirts have indeed become iconic of America, in particular of working-class America, its toughness and masculinity. This symbolism began to develop in the 1930s, when Hollywood movies

even as I grow old and spend more time in hotel bars and art galleries. The 501 style is itself out of date: the waist is too high. And yet I will not give them up. They are me, dated or not. And they are a perfect match for black jackets and loose shirts, or tight T-shirts and black boots. You can ride your bicycle in them, in the rain. And I don't mind letting people know with my clothing that I'm a little bit odd. ❧

became the most popular entertainment all over the world. For the first time in European history it became widely popular to look like someone of a lower, rather than of a higher, social class. Thugs of all kinds, American gangsters in particular, were being glamorized by the movies: for the first time underclasses and underworlds began to influence high fashion.

After the Second World War, the Marshall Plan of financial aid, plus the massive selling of U.S. military surplus clothing across Europe, furthered the Americanization of international fashion. To look casual, or even rough, became cool; it carried connotations of American macho and freedom. This was the beginning of the schism that we still experience today between "street" fashion and conservative dressing.

The 1954 film *The Wild One*, starring Marlon Brando as a motorcycle gang leader, cemented the association between hoodlum dress and the romanticism of working class or outlaw life. The bikers' uniform of blue jeans, T-shirt, and zippered leather motorcycle jacket became an instant signifier of a certain kind of masculine cool, and remains unchanged to this day. The horizontal-striped T-shirt worn in the movie by Chino the biker became a famous signifier of criminality as well: the San Francisco Hells Angels chapter leader Frank Sadilek bought the T-shirt and wore it when meeting police officials. In the 1970s, the seminal punk-rock group the Ramones were still wearing variations on this uniform, including the regulation horizontal-striped T-shirt under their zippered jackets.

Rebel Without a Cause appeared in 1955, furthering the glamorous associations between T-shirts, leather jackets, knife fights, and male sexuality. It is often said (although never proved) that T-shirt sales soared after James Dean wore one throughout the film.

The director Jean-Luc Godard signalled the alien Americanness of his heroine in *Breathless* (1959) by putting actress Jean Seberg in a T-shirt advertising the New York *Herald Tribune*. Everything about her image was calculated to evoke the brash New World, from her cropped, boyish haircut, to her trousers, to the name of the newspaper.

The fact that she was wearing advertising was also meant, I think, to connote American brass. For the primary modern function of the T-shirt – as advertising billboard – is also a largely American story, a product of the energetic capitalism that has proved far more powerful an imperial force, in the long run, than even the Royal Navy.

There are two kinds of advertising now popular on T-shirts: one is for a product or place. If you wear a T-shirt that says "Hard Rock Cafe London," you are boasting of having visited a large city; if you wear one that says "Chicago Bulls," you are proclaiming an emotional allegiance; if you wear one that says "Star Wars," you are proclaiming a specific

The smoking jacket

I am surprised there has been no revival of the shorter silk jacket called a **smoking jacket**, a nineteenth-century essential that a wealthy man kept in his billiards room or library – the sanctum where he and his male friends smoked. The point was to take your dinner jacket off after dinner, so as not to smoke it up, and put on the smoking jacket once you entered the smoking room. After your cigar, you left it in there. It was acceptable to entertain in the smoking jacket, which was short and heavy (for warmth), often quilted or brocade, with silk facing on the lapels, double-breasted or belted. It is out of the smoking jacket that the contemporary dinner jacket or black tie evolved. Yves Saint Laurent revived the smoking jacket in the 1960s – but for women's wear. Giorgio Armani designed several suits ☞

cultural sensibility. The other kind of advertising is for the manufacturer of the T-shirt itself. If you wear a T-shirt that says Hilfiger or Nike, you are trying to associate yourself with a brand, which is a much more nebulous kind of societal positioning. You are boasting of having the same taste as the Tommy Hilfiger corporation, and perhaps some of its power and glamour, such as it is.

As you can guess, I am less than sympathetic to attempts to express one's individuality through the wearing of advertising for clothing manufacturers. I am opposed to any and all logos on T-shirts, or anywhere else.

T-shirts are great for relaxing in cabins and on beaches. And they can look chic under casual suits and jackets, as long as they are new, unfaded, crisp and clean. Stick to solid colours and you will be resisting the deep voodoo of branding.

Lounging at Home

I know that separation from one's childhood is painful. So believe me, it gives me no pleasure to wrench you from your belted trenchcoat, your university knapsack. I do it with the grim determination of Matron ripping off a bandage: a brief sting, but it's for your own long-term good.

And so to the delicate issue at hand: it's about your velour bathrobe. It is blue polyester (am I right?), no lapels. It is the kind you have had since your sheets had cowboys or spaceships on them, and you still find it practical: you throw it in the washer *and* the dryer, no problem.

Velour bathrobes are for guys who value comfort above all, who don't think it matters what you wear when watching the game, when there's no one but your wife or girlfriend to see, and she doesn't care what you look like, right? (Just as you don't care what *she* looks like, right?) The French call a comfort-obsessed guy a *pantouflard*. The term comes from the word for slippers (*pantoufles*); the -*ard* ending is, needless to say, pejorative. The French are tough on such things.

Not that I am opposed to comfort or lounging or watching games, particularly in fiercest winter. Bathrobes (or dressing gowns in Britain) can be the most luxurious and elegant of apparel. I have no objection to heavy white terry cotton and its Hollywoody connotations of poolsides and four-star hotels. In summer, a certain pleasure can be had by stepping onto the front step barefoot to pick up the paper in a blinding white fine cotton or linen robe, as if you lived in a perpetual spa.

But it is winter. And a soft cashmere robe (picture it: navy, with rope piping, over your silk pyjamas, brandy snifter at hand) is as beautiful and fastidious a garment as the finest business suit. More sensual still than the cashmere is the heavy silk dressing gown (the slightly ribbed jacquard weave, not charmeuse), which has the advantage of being printed with subtle patterns: a fine dot or a florid

in the 1990s with a smoking jacket feel (high-gorged, contrasting facing on the lapels), and dandies at black-tie events sometimes substitute a velvet, double-breasted jacket for a black one. But the only place to find a genuine at-home smoking jacket is in a vintage shop – just the place for the closet Sherlock Holmes. You may have to tolerate that musty vintage odour – but it's a better fate than velour. ❧

paisley marks you as at least an art collector, if not an actual artist.

Consider, before you buy, whether you are a lapels or no-lapels man: the lapel-less robe has a Japanese kimono look, very modern but rather spare, connoting to me a desert modernism, all stark white apartments and cacti. Whereas the wide lapels on the traditional robe are baroque: they match a certain clutter (books and wine bottles), rooms in dark colours, worn leather sofas. I venture that the lapel-wearing man is a single-malt man rather than a vegetable-juice man.

These can be expensive items. Silk ones can be had for under two hundred dollars, but the more luxurious cashmere robes start at around three hundred dollars. I feel that they are worth spending money on: you will feel comforted by quality, by warmth, and by softness when you need that brandy in front of the fire as your lover gratefully burns your old one.

CHAPTER NINE

UNDERWEAR

A man becomes the creature of his uniform.
– NAPOLEON I

Each style of underpants comes with its own mythology: one can refer to boxers or briefs or tighty-whiteys as a kind of shorthand, a code for types of man. The significance of these things has been highly exaggerated by all the commentary on them, which has created a kind of generalized anxiety, a repressed giggle, around the whole subject of male underwear. So, first of all, let's all just relax. The kind of underwear you wear really says very little about you, except what you find comfortable. You can wear what you want without fear of judgment.

My interest, however, is not in what you find comfortable, but in what will make you look the sexiest when you disrobe in front of a Swedish model.

But first, let's catalogue those mythic types.

The cliché about the loose-**boxer**-wearing man is that he is a guy's guy. He's not too concerned about these candy-ass questions of fancy dressing. He says his cotton boxers are great because they give him a lot of room to swing around in. (The implication is that his equipment is so huge it needs vast unimpeded swinging arcs.) He likes to wear his boxers under his velour bathrobe and watch TV. He likes to slap his jiggling belly while he watches football. If he likes his boxers printed with humorous symbols – happy faces, dollar signs – he is even more all of these things.

The silk-boxer-wearing man is not like this. His is a time-honoured mix of conservatism and sensuality. Winston Churchill was said to have worn pink silk boxers. And no one called him a pussy.

The Y-front **brief** guy has complicated sub-clichés to go into. There are two associations here: (1) Very unattractive fat guy in front of TV. Briefs will have two colours: contrasting seams and fabric. Or they will be stained. (2) Super-hot muscle guy in gay phone-sex ad. His Y-front briefs are shining pristine white. (This is the cliché that gave rise to the phrase "tighty-whiteys.")

The second cliché owes a great deal to Calvin Klein's famous ad campaign of the 1980s. This was the moment at which the old-fashioned Y-front brief was transformed from image of dull tastelessness to image of sexuality. It was also the moment at which men looked up at vast billboards

"The cliché about the LOOSE-BOXER-WEARING man is that HE is a GUY'S guy."

of naked, muscular, hairless guys and felt, for the first time, insecure about their bodies, just walking along the street.

The tight, white, Y-front brief is still a staple fantasy of gay pornography, probably because it is so quintessentially masculine, and also so boyish.

Next: the **fitted boxer**. This is a relatively recent development, and tends to signal the North American urban sophisticate – the straight guy who is nevertheless somewhat vain and works out a lot. This new strain of underwear owes a lot to the relatively recent acceptance of new fabrics in men's underwear: the stretchy and the shiny, spandex and microfibre, have long been considered too sensual, too feminine, for men, who supposedly should only accept rough fabrics next to their most sensitive parts.

And finally, in our hierarchy of dandyisms, comes the **fitted brief** – the brief with no Y-front, no thick seams. It too usually contains some stretchy material to make it more clingy. This is, in cliché, the terrain of the European dandy, the guy who has no questions or insecurities about his masculinity, who indeed has not even considered this question.

Of course, all these myths are just that. Wearing tighty-whiteys does not make you gay any more than wearing a spandex thong makes you European. So let us consider, instead, the aesthetic and practical advantages of these designs.

Women still like the classic loose boxer: it looks masculine and flatters even the out-of-shape figure.

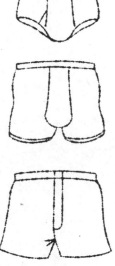

Briefs, fitted boxers, and boxers

However, some men may find that it contains too much fabric, which bunches uncomfortably in the groin and at the waist. I myself hate to feel I am wearing a large and cumbersome garment under my trousers; they feel like diapers. Furthermore, some men may find that the unimpeded swinging of the private parts can actually be uncomfortable, particularly during vigorous activity. They want some support.

Hence the fitted boxer or brief. The advantage of the boxer-cut over the brief-cut is that even tight jeans will not reveal its telltale seams across your buttocks. The outline of briefs is more likely to be visible through your trousers, if your trousers are at all tight (or if you put your hands in your pockets, thus stretching the fabric over your big ass).

Briefs are practical because minimal: the less fabric there is under your clothing, the more comfortable you will feel, particularly in warm situations. But, as I've said, there are prejudices against briefs, particularly among North American women, who tend to giggle at the sight of them: they associate them with sitcom clichés of skinny guys with long hair called Lorenzo, who wear a lot of gold jewellery and unbuttoned shirts.

I am a big backer of the fitted boxer as a sexy and modern compromise. They look particularly good if you are in good shape, as they reveal the figure. And there is no earthly reason to be afraid of those sensual fabrics – those clingy microfibres in particular. They are comfortable and soft.

As to colour, shorts or briefs in blinding white are certainly sexy. The problem is making sure that they are in fact blinding white – if you go out on a date which you expect will end in some intimacy, for example, you had better make sure you put those white things on the very moment before you step out the door. This concern explains why black is an increasingly popular colour in men's underwear. It looks just as sexy as white.

There is thong underwear for men, and there is no reason to sneer or giggle at it. It is useful for extremely tight trousers, as it eliminates any visible underwear lines. It also gives maximum support, so it perks up your package.

I am informed by female friends of the rising popularity of the no-underwear-at-all option, usually embraced by actors, would-be actors, and heavy drinkers (apparently often one and the same). It is meant to appear daring, because nonchalant (as if you simply couldn't be bothered to find your shorts today), and therefore masculine. It carries some disadvantages: you can embarrass people to the point of encouraging sexual-harassment charges if you walk around at work with your equipment very visibly swinging under a thin or loose pair of trousers. There is some information about you that your colleagues don't want to possess. Furthermore,

"The NO-UNDERWEAR-AT-ALL option is usually EMBRACED by actors, WOULD-BE actors, and heavy DRINKERS."

without underwear you will stain your expensive trousers with all kinds of embarrassing leakages, and this also can be visible to your colleagues. So be daring at your own risk.

Swimsuits

No continent loathes and fears the male **bikini** swimsuit more than North America does. Mention "guy in bikini swimsuit" and brows crinkle, teeth are bared, the word *disgusting* is spat out. I can understand this among straight men – any overt fetishizing of the male body, when not disguised as sport, is suspect to them – but the way *women* squeal and squirm about the horror of the Lycra-clad male makes me wonder sometimes if they aren't just as repressed and body-loathing as we are.

I realize that the scorn of the bikini has as much to do with recent fashion as with sexuality. For some reason, one cannot picture an Olympic swimmer; hear the word *bikini* and immediately a shaggy older guy with a beer gut, aviator glasses, and a leathery tan comes to mind. The bikini connotes the seventies, and so the people we remember wearing them are guys whose fashion sense has not changed since then.

However, there is a paradox here, because fashion has, for some fifteen years now, been obsessed with the sixties and seventies. What with all the bell-bottoms and sideburns and *Wallpaper* and *Vice* magazines, one would think the bikini would be

"No continent LOATHES and FEARS the male BIKINI swimsuit more than NORTH AMERICA does."

making a triumphant ironic-cool return. In fact, Gucci's bathing suits of the mid-nineties *were* relentlessly *Wallpaper*-like; chocolate brown, tight **trunks** cut high on the leg and high on the waist, rather like the cut of Batman's groin-piece, for wearing in your own private Burt Lancaster movie. Not quite bikinis, but very nostalgic and very form-fitting.

These vaguely kitschy high-fashion items – worn only by the kind of man who would consider spending over three hundred dollars on a bathing suit; that is, a very in-shape man – are still going strong in the Deep End, among the expensive, fashion-forward designers. They are still making short square-cuts, and the occasional Batman-style bikini with a very high waistband and a few laces on the front. The references in all these designs are, interestingly, not to the seventies but to the fifties. These are the bathing suits worn by the heroes of American beach movies (Frankie Avalon, Elvis Presley) and Biblical epics (the chariot-drivers and gladiators of *Spartacus* and *Ben Hur*). They connote extreme masculinity – but the references are now ironic.

Many less expensive designers are now making flattering **square-cut bikinis,** or **"fitted" boxers.** But I admit that they do only really work on a well-toned abdomen. Which is why the modern conservative macho man still tends toward baggy **shorts** with a drawstring waist. I find these boring. I don't mind exaggeratedly large, knee-length surfer-shorts in ripstop nylon; these are the mark of the hipster or the youth. It's the compromise guys that dismay me; the guys in short but loose running shorts. Sometimes they have a little Nike logo or three Adidas stripes down the side. These are the guys who simply don't want to think about it; they can't face taking the plunge into actually buying a bathing suit. And so they end up looking even more seventies-retro than the bikini guys. Nothing reminds one of Junior High more than those little Adidas running shorts. Furthermore, trunks that are both loose *and* short often end up being indecent.

Baggy is fine, as long as it's cool baggy. The swimsuit of the crop-headed, skateboard-owning under-thirty is, invariably, a pair of surfer shorts. These are long and rugged and heavy, made of ripstop nylon, like a backpack. They are often vaguely techno-looking, with pockets with Velcro closures and mesh plackets, and lots of contrasting stitching. If you're going to go baggy, go all the way, and look young and confident rather than safely noncommittal. Go short and tight or long and loose. There is no middle ground.

CHAPTER TEN

OUTERWEAR

The trick of wearing mink is to look as though you were wearing a cloth coat. The trick of wearing a cloth coat is to look as though you are wearing mink.

– PIERRE BALMAIN

U.S. vice president Dick Cheney showed true frat-boy panache when he wore a fur-hooded parka, snow boots, and a wool toque (complete with some sort of advertising logo), to the extremely sombre ceremonies marking the fiftieth anniversary of the liberation of Auschwitz, in January 2005. It was a cold day, and snowing, and the ceremony took place outside. I suppose he thought the world would admire his practicality. All the other dignitaries – including all the presidents and prime ministers of Europe – managed to tolerate the cold in dark wool overcoats, black shoes, and black fur hats or black felt hats with brims. The event was, basically, a memorial service, a form of funeral, for hundreds of thousands of people. This was not the right place for demonstrating America's famously casual dress code. To the European press, the vice president's dress seemed shockingly disrespectful. Outraged editorials appeared on both sides of the Atlantic. To me, it seemed both disrespectful and smug, even boastful – as if Cheney were making some sort of point about the insouciance of Americans, and possibly about their egalitarian traditions.

This is something Americans and Canadians often don't understand about dress: it's not all about you. What you wear shows what you think of the people around you. You dress, on many occasions, particularly sombre and formal ones, to show respect for others.

In cold countries, brightly coloured parkas and puffy down jackets may indeed be more practical, and warmer, than classic wool overcoats. But they are casual. They are inappropriate for wear with a suit and tie. You may think you look young and hip, or outdoorsy, on your way to work in a bank or a law office, hiding your suit with a puffy ski jacket. You are right about the young part: you will look very young indeed. The parka-over-the-suit thing is one of those undergraduate habits young business-men are often reluctant to break, just as they resist parting with their bright nylon university knapsacks.

It is time to graduate. Let us get you a grown-up coat.

The classic men's overcoat has not changed its shape much since the 1870s, but the lengths vary

"This is something AMERICANS and Canadians often don't UNDERSTAND about DRESS: it's NOT all about YOU."

minutely from decade to decade. The **balmacaan** style, named after an estate near Inverness, Scotland, has a small, shirt-like collar, and sometimes an A-line silhouette, a slight widening of the skirts as they approach the ground.

It also has, most importantly, a kind of sleeve called a **raglan** sleeve, which means that the sleeve is sewn to the collar rather than to the shoulder. This style of coat was designed by Lord Raglan for his troops fighting in the Crimean War in the 1850s.

Raglan sleeve coat

Balmacaan coats used to be made only of tweed, but now the term refers to any coat in this pattern. These coats reach to just above or just below the knee – but just above is the hipper length today. Medium-length and single-breasted is in. Short coats look rather schoolboy-like, which makes them seem less formal. I still think they look great with a suit. If you are wealthy enough to afford more than one overcoat, you may have one short daily-wear coat in navy, camel, or dark brown, and then indulge in one longer, black formal coat with a velvet or fur collar. The contrasting fabric in the collar means that the coat is called a **chesterfield** style, named after the Earl of Chesterfield, who wore such coats in the 1830s. He was himself copying French aristocrats of the previous century, who had taken to wearing black velvet strips in their collars as a discreet sign of mourning after the execution in 1793 of Louis XVI.

Square shoulders and notch lapels are still acceptable, of course. Forward designers are now making variations on the 1960s Carnaby Street–style of overcoat (which was itself a copy of Edwardian patterns), with a nipped waist – an hourglass silhouette – and even a hacking pocket. But you still can't go wrong with the old-fashioned straight line from top to bottom.

Solid colours (black, grey, navy, camel, or brown) are safer than patterns. Sheep wool is the warmest acceptable fabric; lighter, more expensive cashmere is often woven in for softness. Many coat fabrics now contain a small percentage of nylon, for shape; this will actually make your coat last a little longer, so it is not to be scorned, although such a coat will not be as warm as the all-wool.

In Nancy Mitford's 1949 novel, *Love in a Cold Climate*, the delicate dandy Cedric is assaulted at a magazine kiosk by the conservative Uncle Matthew for wearing an overcoat with contrasting piping around the seams. "You'd never think that buying *Vogue* magazine could be so dangerous," remarks Cedric.

But all such deviations *are* dangerous, as Cedric well knew. I myself feel some of Uncle Matthew's ire when I see a portly man in a snug *belted* overcoat. What man, outside those with tall, Pierce Brosnan-esque physiques, which is to say what normal man, could possibly think he looks attractive swaddled in miles of dense wool, his thick middle not only rendered thicker but actually accentuated by the heavily knotted belt, in a silhouette like a bathrobe? Am I the only one who finds the wrapped-up-parcel look infantilizing, like appearing in public in your jammies?

The conventional wisdom is that belts are appropriate for raglan sleeves and not square shoulders. The idea is that the sloping raglan shoulder makes the middle of the coat appear wider. In order to keep the silhouette narrow, the belt cinches the coat at the waist. This, however, does not apply to so many modern coats, which maintain both raglan sleeves and a narrow silhouette. Furthermore, big shoulders are not necessary for the contemporary man.

And what's the point of walking around with the coat buttoned but the belt loose and flapping, as so many men do? Readers of this book do not flap. They never have trailing appendages. They dress in sleek, straight lines, like modern buildings and mid-sixties Mercedes.

"Overly LONG overcoats are PASSÉ."

Overly long overcoats are also passé. The coat that hangs close to your ankles is a dramatic, Wild-West-gunfighter sort of look (as popularized in the *Matrix* movies, and later by the teenage murderers of Columbine High School), which also succeeds in rendering a short man even shorter. It dwarfs those under six feet tall. And perhaps wanting to dress like a science-fiction character is not the most mature of aspirations.

Fur

Vicuña: The mother of all coats

There is a scene in *Sunset Boulevard* in which the aging and insane actress Norma Desmond takes her young protege shopping for clothes. He has a choice between a fine camel-hair coat and an ultra-fine vicuña – a coat made from the fleece of a nearly extinct miniature Andean camel. "Since the lady's paying," murmurs the salesman in his ear, "why not take the vicuña?" The guilty anti-hero looks troubled. To accept the lunatic luxury of the vicuña coat is to accept that he has sold his soul. The vicuña coat represents his moral decay.

I remember thinking it was a sign that Canada was a grown-up country when I first saw, six or seven years ago, a vicuña coat on sale in downtown Toronto: finally, we were decadent. It was at Harry Rosen, on Bloor Street. The coat was by Brioni of Italy. The wool – each ☞

Fur is a delicate topic, so just avoid it if you are sensitive. I have no interest in the moral debate, only in the aesthetic. And I love fur. I don't even mind fur to excess – big bushy coats that you associate with 1920s millionaires at Harvard football games (with bow tie and boater), even though this affectation will probably invite ridicule from cautious modern people. A fur coat on a man speaks of vanity to the point of narcissism, it speaks of confidence to the point of arrogance: a fur coat says *fuck you*.

I have no problem with this. But if you want to avoid the disdain of the modern people (that puny breed!), you do have some toned-down options to consider. There are coats of black lambswool with a textured, shiny surface, which are almost as flamboyant. And there is a currently fashionable option: the wool coat with the fur collar.

The new breed – and I'm talking about coats from such designers as Gucci, Comme des Garçons and Baldessarini – replace the sober fur collar of the classic chesterfield with a preposterous fur mane. The new chesterfields sport luxuriant matted growths around the neck and lapels. (The fur is either real or fun, depending on the designer, so those with moral scruples can still participate in fashion.) At best, the look is one of nineteenth-century privilege – the kind of thing an Italian banker would wear in a Guido Crepax cartoon. At worst, it's pimpy – something to wear with gold chains and a wide-brimmed hat. It's certainly a far cry from the full-length fur coat of the 1920s Harvard man, at once more restrained and more glamorous. I encourage excess and flamboyance, particularly in the grey winter. Such indulgence looks powerful, sensual, and whimsical at the same time: in other words, manly.

Raincoats

There was once a function to all the straps and buckles and flaps on the classic **trench coat**. It was a military coat, designed by Thomas Burberry (the manufacturer who perfected the type of tough, water-resistant gabardine used in most raincoats today) for British officers in the First World War. The coat was double-breasted and long for warmth, the belt's D-rings were for attaching hand grenades, and the epaulettes had two functions: displaying insignia, and holding in place the shoulder strap of the holster (the "Sam Browne"). Have you ever wondered why the most military-looking of trench coats have an extra flap over the right shoulder only? It's to cushion your rifle butt, of course, when you are shooting.

And what do all the military appurtenances connote today? Do they indicate battle-readiness? Do they convey the laconic derring-do of Bogart in the last scene of *Casablanca*?

In fact, no. The belted trench coat has much gentler, safer connotations now. It means Dad. It

animal yields only about 250 grams of fleece, but they are sheared live – was milled by Loro Piana. It was a 42 regular. It was very soft. And it cost $29,995. (I talked to a salesman at the store who estimated they had about a fifty-fifty chance of selling it. Not everyone got to try it on, only tycoons with a history of spending in the store.) You can order your own vicuna coat from Brioni, or you can order one made-to-measure from the best tailors in any large city, and it will probably actually cost you less, because there is no brand name on it. You can probably get away with a vicuna coat for about twenty-five-thousand dollars. Or for nothing, if the lady is paying. ๛

means minivan. It means junior sales rep. To me it suggests a slightly flustered guy, because you usually see them unbuttoned, with assorted patches and straps flapping. It cries out for a pair of nice practical rubber overshoes and a Samsonite attaché case. Either that or an ironic seventies-lover, with aviator shades and a tennis hat. (This type of dandy tends to go for the *suede* trench coat.)

The trench-coat era has passed. It is time to abandon the military symbols. The confident man does not need them, just as he does not need the cowboy excess of the long, Wild West "dusters" that are sold as raincoats in stores with "Creek" and "Ridge" and "Outback" in their names. You know the ones, the dark brown, rough-surfaced ones that go down to your ankles and have a big scalloped yoke over the shoulders at the back. They are perfectly appropriate accompaniments to pointy boots and Stetsons, as long as you are actually riding a horse.

Nor do grown-ups wear bright Gore-Tex rain-slickers of the Patagonia or Mountain Equipment Co-op variety over anything but hiking boots. (I often wonder – for I have never actually bought such a thing – if Day-Glo Gore-Tex rain shells come with a free beard, maybe an instant spray-on beard in a can.) Private-school boys who wear Barbours (the expensively rugged green oilskin English hunting jacket) over their suits, even when they are in town – to show that they are country folk at heart – are being pretentious.

For urban environments, a simpler, subtler, and lighter coat is more suitable. In keeping with the narrow-silhouette fashion of the times, modern raincoats are gabardine, **single-breasted,** and plain. They have small, shirt-style collars (like the balmacaan coat); if they have lapels they are short and narrow. They have no belt, epaulettes, back yoke, or other distracting details. They hang straight down like a cylinder. Even the buttons are usually hidden by a placket. They usually have raglan sleeves.

Don't feel that you are restricted to dark colours here: light grey and tan are no less conservative, in raincoats, than are charcoal and navy. In fact, a dove grey raincoat, in soft spring rain or crisp autumn sun, can be as elegant and romantic a garment as a shining suit of armour.

Umbrellas

Umbrellas may strike you as aesthetically straightforward. But they are a part of your attire, and as such are delicate terrain, full of hidden signifiers and historical significance.

The word comes from the Latin for shade (*umbra*). An Englishman named Thomas Coryate, writing of a visit to Italy in 1611, was the first to describe these strange shades, made of strong leather, being carried by horsemen as protection from the

"For URBAN environments, a SIMPLER, SUBTLER, and LIGHTER coat is more SUITABLE."

sun. Over the years they grew lighter, and by the nineteenth century English-speakers were distinguishing between the umbrella, for rain, and the parasol, for sun. They became fetish objects in the twentieth century, particularly in rainy Britain, where the tightly furled umbrella became a class signifier. The umbrella, along with the briefcase, newspaper, and bowler hat, became the quintessential symbol of the man who worked in "the City," the financial district of London.

The rules for this uniform were strict: the umbrella was always to be rolled tightly as a cigar, thin as a rapier. The little folding umbrellas of North American men, the ones that always seem to be flapping and getting caught in similarly flapping trench-coat belts, would bring shudders to English high society. I knew a financial executive in London in the 1970s who always carried an immaculately furled umbrella, sleek as a piece of licorice, and kept another less perfect one in his car – for when it rained.

What to look for in an umbrella? First, the short, folding variety may seem practical and light, but it is undignified. If you must have one (if you are actually travelling, say, and want to be able to pack it), then keep it wrapped and in your briefcase. The proper umbrella is a full-length one, and it is black. Now, if you are confident, you may experiment with subtle greys, navies, and pinstripes, but this is Advanced Class territory. The extra-large umbrella with bright red-and-black stripes, or some sort of humorous slogan, is fun for the class clown, and of course we all appreciate those who make life more amusing. (Girls really like the class clown, but only as a friend.)

Handles are a better place for the expression of whimsy: there is something elegant about a man with an antique carved wooden handle in the shape of a duck's head. Leather-wrapped handles are also nice to the touch.

The differences between cheap ones and expensive ones are not visible. They all look basically the same. But pricier ones tend to weigh less, an important consideration when carrying a briefcase and hailing a cab. Cheap ones will explode in high winds. And look for a steel tip on the pointy end. (Make sure you let the umbrella dry before furling it, or the steel will rust.)

The problem with expensive umbrellas is that you lose them. As soon as it stops raining you forget you had one. I lose about one a month, and so only buy twenty-five-dollar jobs from large department stores (which look perfectly fine). Some entrepreneurial genius will take my advice and set up an umbrella home-delivery service that provides regular bunches of umbrellas – say three a month – to busy households between April and November.

> "The PROBLEM with EXPENSIVE umbrellas is that you LOSE them."

Hats

Judging from movies, you'd think some kind of global hat treaty went into effect on the stroke of midnight on January 1, 1960. In the fifties, every man wears a suit and a hat every day of his life, then suddenly the sixties begin and nobody does. It wasn't as sudden as that, of course, and in fact the key date in the mass extinction of hats is often thought to be John F. Kennedy's inauguration in 1961, to which he went hatless, shocking the nation.

Actually, like so many legends, this one is only partly true. Kennedy wore the traditional top hat while sitting in the stands during the ceremony, but he removed it – along with his overcoat – when it came time to deliver his speech. The hat enabled people to recognize him in the crowd from afar, but when he stood alone at the microphone, his bare head gave the impression of youthful vigour.

Why fashions suddenly appear or disappear is often hard to fathom, but mass trends can frequently be traced to the early adoption by some kind of celebrity. And in the case of men's hats, the most influential have been on the heads of heads of state. Examples: Edward VII, when he was Prince of Wales, frequented the pre-jet-set trendy German spa town of Bad Homburg, where he took to wearing a jaunty Tyrolean felt hat with a turned-up brim. Such a hat is to this day called a **Homburg**, although its conjunction with the town is coincidental.

Similarly, the so-called **Panama** is not and was not ever made in Panama, but was famously sported there by Theodore Roosevelt on inspecting the new canal in 1906. The true Panama is handwoven in

Ecuador (go figure), from the fine straw of the jipi-japa plant. This straw is water-resistant and flexible: the hat made from it can be rolled up and put in a hat-tube. My favourite style of Panama is the classic: called the Optimo, it doesn't have a dented crown, like most hats, but a ridge running lengthwise over the crown.

(from top) Fedora, trilby, and Panama hats

Having said that, however, I admit I am not a big fan of hats generally. The classic gentleman's hat – basically a **fedora**, a felt hat with a rim which can be "snapped," turned up or down – now looks deliberately retro and eccentric. Yes, fedoras and **trilbys** (the soft brown English felt hat with a narrower brim, worn at horse races and in the country) are made of beaver or rabbit fur, and so are warm in winter. They may be practical, but they simply look silly. If you are old, they make you look older; if you are young, they make you look as if you are trying to look old, which is no better. Young guys wearing old guys' hats are like young guys smoking pipes or wearing pocket watches or taking snuff: these are the clever, nerdy guys with interesting record collections. Women want to hang out with them at lunch, but not at dinner.

When the temperature is below zero, one is forced to wear a hat for purely practical reasons, and I am afraid there are few attractive options. At this point one must just bite the bullet and look like a dork. So go all the way and be warm: wear a full-on fur hat with flaps you can tie up at the crown for a more dressy look. (Rabbit is as good as any other fur for warmth, and rabbits are in no danger of extinction.)

Summer also has its own practical demands. As the ozone depletes, it is increasingly dangerous to walk around for hours in blazing sun. Here the straw hat is useful, and can have its own debonair charm, although it's a tricky business: the very wide-brimmed straw hats, especially when worn with casual wear, can make one look like the organizer of a rural craft fair. And a real Panama, even when worn with a lovely linen suit, can carry with it at best a whiff of the ageing roué and at worst a hint of the wannabe Central American gangster.

Consider instead the straw **porkpie**, an oval hat with a totally flat top and a brim turned up all the way around; it's a little less of the plantation owner, a little more of the Impressionist café-concert. Your goal is to attain the frilly glamour of turn-of-the-century paintings of summer leisure – dancing Renoir boatmen, picnicking Manet aesthetes. Edwardian images of summer always seem to involve straw hats, but flat-topped urban ones, not American wide-open-spaces ones.

Indeed, you may even have the courage to plunge into deep dandyism with a genuine straw **boater** – a stiff, flat-topped hat made of lacquered sennit straw, as worn from the 1880s to the 1930s. (A **canotier** is the same thing: it means oarsman or gondolier.) You have seen boaters on Buster Keaton and Maurice Chevalier; my father was issued one at his colonial

British school as part of his cricket uniform (for off the field, of course), with a school crest on the band. Boaters are still made by the oldest hat manufacturers, and can be ordered from specialty hat stores.

I am not speaking here of hipster hats: fuzzy white Kangol caps, black tennis hats (you know, the kind Gilligan wore) with words like *Groovy* on them, leopardskin cowboy hats with curled-up sides . . . these are for the Advanced Class and are usually proclamations of specific social or musical tastes. People have such powerful pride in such hats – largely because they are declarations of defiance, of would-be nonconformism, of insecure individuality – that I wouldn't dare to interfere. I won't attempt to rip your favourite ratty club-going toque from you. Indeed, silliness is often what makes these hats so beloved.

I myself have a black tennis hat with a red star on it. It comes down so low over my eyes I can hardly see out. When I put it on I channel the personality of a fourteen-year-old drug dealer called Scooter, who is a very hyper individual and who always seems to be looking for his friend Veeper. I find this change of persona invigorating when I go out to techno clubs, and I don't care who laughs at me. In this hat, I am Scooter.

Finally, a note on regular felt cowboy hats: I do not describe regular felt cowboy hats because they do not exist in my universe.

Ditto for baseball caps.

Tilt it forward

The most important tip for the wearing of all these hats is the one which is most frequently ignored in North America: wear it forward on the head. Even more forward than you want, the lower the better. Do not display any of your forehead: the front brim should sit just above your eyes. If you wear it back on your head you will look like a character from Mark Twain. The farther forward, the more urban and grown-up you will look.

Scarves

Like ties and pocket squares, the winter scarf is a site for the display of colour and personality in the otherwise dark and uniform facade of winter coats and suits. So let us cast off the sensible plaids and variations on grey. Flamboyance is welcome in scarves. There are few more masculine sights than an elegant wool overcoat – navy, charcoal, or camel – set off with a dazzling silk scarf, printed in paisley, maybe even tasselled.

Experiment with ethnicity here: long raw-silk scarves from Nepal, shiny Indonesian rayon print things . . . all can be matched, by the expert, with a sober suit and overcoat. Whimsy is encouraged.

Wool scarves can be lovely too, as long as they are extremely fine – of high-twist, worsted yarn, not nubbly woollen yarn – and woven, like a suit fabric, rather than knitted. Yes, current fashion has popularized knitted wool scarves again, but they are finer than the ones your mother made you; they tend to have thin, multicoloured stripes and look vaguely academic, as if you are an adjunct professor from Milan.

Big and long scarves are dramatic only if they are fine: the goofy, lengthy, knitted, striped, tasselled scarf that fun undergrads wear with vintage coats and canvas basketball shoes is cute, but so is a class clown (you remember what the girls think of him). Women's scarves and shawls in rich colours, if folded lengthwise to make them long rather than wide,

"Like TIES and pocket squares, the WINTER SCARF is a site for the DISPLAY of colour and PERSONALITY."

actually look great on men. Nobody will recognize a **pashmina** shawl as such on a man if you fold it lengthwise and wrap it like a scarf. (Pashminas are made from a blend of silk and the hair of a rare mountain goat, and are exquisitely soft and warm.)

With formal wear, nothing is more sensual and elegant than the classic **white silk** scarf. When white silk ages, it grows yellow – don't throw it out. A man with an antique silk scarf is an interesting man, no matter how ratty it may seem to some. Yellow silk is class.

Bags

The knapsack was a practical invention. It enabled one to carry hardy rations – cured beef and hard-tack, I imagine – on arduous mountain hikes and leave one's hands free for scrabbling in the rock and bracken, whatever bracken is. Made of khaki canvas, it is a perfect aesthetic match with lederhosen. Made of the more modern nylon webbing, it comes in happy colours and with a university logo, and is meant for carrying your Psych 100 textbook while you ride your mountain bike to happy pubs.

Why, then, do you see young lawyers marching about downtown in new suits and shiny shoes with the old university-logo knapsack slung over one shoulder? They have conformed in every aspect of the uniform, they have even begun to take pride and joy in fine clothes, and yet they fiercely retain this one youthful accessory to prove (to whom?) that they still ride mountain bikes, that they still have their hands free.

It looks dumb for a couple of reasons: (1) nylon webbing is the nastiest, least sensual substance ever created; (2) the straps over your shoulders pull your suit all out of line.

Not that you have to conform by carrying a heavy, sharp-edged boxy briefcase that doesn't hold a squash racket and weighs more empty than your knapsack did full. You can compromise by having, for example, a soft black or brown leather briefcase with a shoulder strap, which you can sling over your back when you clip up your trouser legs and hop on your bicycle for the trip home. (Men in suits on bicycles, by the way, look debonair. Ask any woman.) When arriving at a serious meeting, you unclip the strap, stuff it inside, and carry the now grown-up briefcase by the handle.

These bags are unfortunately not cheap: they start at around three hundred dollars. But they can be very luxurious to handle and as they wear they look more distinguished and academic. Make sure yours has a shoulder strap and you will never miss your knapsack. If you can't afford one, you can buy, in any office-building concourse, a plain black nylon briefcase with a shoulder strap for around thirty dollars; it is not elegant, but neither is it noticeable.

The trendiest look for those in creative fields is inspired by bicycle couriers and rave fashions: the lurid plastic shoulder bag. Shaped like a briefcase but made of shiny, waterproof, red or yellow PVC and festooned with reflective tape, it's a designer/copywriter/cinematographer look that nods to science fiction but is actually practical as well.

Bags generally are more important these days, as men have more to carry. Cellphones and PDAs will weigh your suit down and tear holes in the linings of the pockets. You don't want to walk around with your pockets stuffed with gear, like some sort of Special Forces commando, right?

This problem has led to the invention of the male purse or manbag, a small oblong leather briefcase, about the size of a steno pad, with a wrist strap, meant to contain wallet, passport, glasses. It looks like a woman's evening clutch, but in plain leather. It was big in Europe in the seventies, and although it never caught on among macho North American males, variations on the conventional briefcase shape are becoming more visible, even in the corridors of power. The line between briefcase and purse is growing finer. Smaller bags, about the size of women's purses, are increasingly seen carried by younger guys, particularly in techno-shiny nylon and other rubbery substances, with tidy individual pockets for phone, iPod, BlackBerry, graphic novel, and rolling papers. Note that these useful totes are cool only if they have a shoulder strap. The leather Europurse with the handle still makes a guy look a little . . . well, not feminine (which can be attractive, particularly to women), but fastidious, fussy, maybe a little small. I still associate them with the overly tanned, overly cologned, over-fifty European gentleman in a silk knit shirt and tinted aviator glasses.

So what to do with all your stuff? Carry as much of it as you can – even your keys – in your briefcase. Slim down your wallet (does it really need every video membership card you ever acquired?). Your change goes in your wallet (leather) or in a *separate* change purse, a small semicircular leather thing that you can get for twenty dollars. Isn't it time you threw out that bright nylon thing with Velcro closures that you bought at a camping store? Better yet, put it inside your nylon knapsack and throw them both out. Along with your undergraduate persona.

SCENT

Every generation laughs at the old fashions,
but follows religiously the new.
- HENRY DAVID THOREAU

o women like it? A difficult question; one hears contradictory answers. North American womankind seems split fifty-fifty on this one: half will say that a man's natural scent cannot be improved upon, that to disguise it with flowery sweetness is a mistake and a distraction, and possibly a sign of vanity. The other half finds an intriguing and original scent to be a sign of sophistication. These splits don't seem to follow any class lines. I'm not sure what explains the difference. Perhaps it's just that women say different things in different moods.

The no-scent faction does have a point. Natural odours contain powerful chemicals. A body's smell will often have a stronger emotional and sexual pull than any visual memory.

But of course the best perfumes do not mask these triggers, they enhance them. Every perfume will smell differently on different bodies: this combination of nature and artifice can be the most powerful stimulus of all.

Furthermore, I believe that the no-scent tradition is dying, as are all conservative views of masculinity. I have been arguing throughout this book that as the New World grows older, it grows more accepting of artifice generally. As more men wear scents, more women are coming to expect it as one more element of the well-dressed man's total package. The wearing of a carefully chosen scent is a sign, particularly to refined urban women, that a man is (a) sensually aware and (b) making an effort to please.

In other words, I encourage the wearing of cologne, but by no means is it mandatory.

All women will agree, as do I, that any perfume must be used sparingly on a man. You want it to be noticed close up; you don't want to overpower a room.

Perfume is an excellent gift for a lover. This is a controversial idea; most people are afraid to give perfumes as gifts. The logic is that scents are so intimate that any interference in the choosing process equals a sort of personality imperialism. This may be true, but the sad fact is that, unless given perfume as a gift, most men would never think of it, much less wear it.

> "Any PERFUME must be used SPARINGLY on a man."

I also think men and women could be a little more daring in what they consider a masculine smell. Old-fashioned men's colognes rely on the following scent categories: citrus, wood, leather, spice, and tobacco. They avoid the floral as a feminine characteristic. Light citrus aromas dominate the vast majority of men's perfumes, and I find them a bore. Why do the manufacturers want us all to smell soapy and fresh and clean, like lemon Pledge? An extreme case is that of Acqua di Parma, an early-twentieth-century perfume that was recently revived in its original formula (and, most importantly, nostalgic packaging) and strenuously marketed to luxury department stores as the essence of tradition and manliness. Its selling point is its very lack of modernity – in other words, it is so unsophisticated as to be crude. It smells like soap and citrus – exactly like the chemical-soaked Wet Nap paper towels in foil packets that you reluctantly open in Greyhound toilets. Acqua di Parma is simply awful.

The other – and infinitely sexier – traditionally male odour is musk, an undefinable, sweetish scent which should really come from a gland of the musk deer or civet cat (but almost never does – it's all synthetic nowadays). The word derives from the Sanskrit for scrotum. That's how manly it is. Combined with clovey spices, it's the basis for the most famously manly smell of all: Old Spice aftershave. Launched in 1957, Old Spice seems cloying and a little sickly today, but it is still, unbelievably, an aphrodisiac for young women. Trust me on this. It has the same deep subliminal effect as shaving cream and undershirts: they get swoony with dad/ childhood nostalgia.

For those who want the dad associations without the flimsiness, a more sophisticated manly-spicy-leathery scent – an upscale Old Spice – is Hermès's Rocabar, a deep and heavy aroma that connotes men's clubs and cigars. This too has a remarkable effect on women, who – in my informal survey – unfailingly call it "manly."

Rocabar, like many spicy scents, which are designated as "orientals" (such as Armani's Black Code, and Guerlain's L'Instant), is manly but not exactly youthful. A few contemporary designers are finally experimenting with "feminine" floral, fruit, and candy scents in men's colognes. Recent colognes by Jean Paul Gaultier, Dolce & Gabbana, and John Varvatos have included vanilla or mint notes, which turn their wearers into walking cakes. Some producers, like Jo Malone, make scents to be worn by both men and women. Don't be afraid of experimenting with these. You'll at least smell distinctive and be remembered.

You will be seeing more non-natural smells listed in perfumes – smells such as nail polish, metal, and burnt rubber. Technological advances (the "micro-extraction method" and the spectroscopic sampling device called the "Headspace") have enabled scientists to synthetically recreate any inorganic smell. The company Demeter has made a series of these "techno fragrances" with names like Rubber, Dirt, and Vinyl. They smell exactly like their names. The point is not to wear them as perfume, but to use them as stimulants, to provoke memories (like Proust's taste of tea and almond cake) or unblock creativity. You can combine them to create an evocative olfactory landscape: wet dog in beach house, cigar on subway.

Perfume manufacturers have also picked up on the trend toward personalizing fragrances. The popularity of aromatherapy has influenced New Agey perfumers such as Aveda and The Body Shop, where you can make your own perfume by asking staff to combine an array of oils or plant extracts (often with poetic names such as Eros and Psyche). The future of perfume might be called U-Mix-It. (And what would make a more moving Christmas gift than a personalized perfume, a kind of character analysis and abstract tone poem, created by a lover solely for the love object?)

CHAPTER TWELVE

HAIR

Hip is the sophistication of the wise
primitive in a giant jungle.
– NORMAN MAILER

*T*his chapter might just as well have come first. Your haircut could easily make your whole look: your head is the first thing people look at. A bad haircut can undermine the most beautiful and fashionable outfit; a slick haircut can make up for a lack of expenditure on clothing. If you really can afford nothing described in this book, then scrape up your pennies and go to a barber; it is all you truly need.

And most men do. Need a barber, that is. If you are at all in doubt about your haircut, cut it shorter. You cannot go wrong with a closely cropped head: it is still the most masculine look, women still find it reassuring, no matter how fashionable the style may seem, and it should be the default option for any man averse to risk.

I admit that I had very long hair long after its zenith of modishness had passed. Like ten years after. But there was no social protest whatever in my decision to grow my hair long, no desire to be associated with hippies or rock musicians or high-school teachers or television producers. I grew my hair long for purely superficial reasons.

It was the mid-eighties, and the great flamboyant aesthetic movement of my youth, punk rock – a resolutely short-haired movement – had fragmented. But punk was basically a movement of fashion, and I retained that sense of fashion being rebellious, anti-suburban. The fashion magazines of the time (radical in themselves, in small university towns) were showing male models in ultra-conservative, dark, double-breasted suits, with manes of glossy hair. It was a sensual look, a nod to androgyny and to dandyism. It was the very opposite of sixties *laissez-faire* (and campus wholesomeness). It was about grooming and vanity and a highly sexual exhibitionism.

My illusions were shattered when I looked in the mirror and realized that I was receding a little in front. So when I tied my hair back I looked like the saddest thing that a man can possibly look like: a rock music critic.

Once I went short, I couldn't believe I hadn't done it years before. People said I looked five years younger. And I entered the fraternity of unsuspicious men. Men – particularly those behind counters in

"If you REALLY can afford NOTHING described in this book, then SCRAPE up your PENNIES and go to a BARBER; it is all you TRULY need."

hardware stores and police stations – were much friendlier. (Unfortunately, female strangers no longer approach me in bars, asking to stroke it.)

I have never looked back. And so it is with some consternation that I must admit that recent fashion is following a disturbing trend. It can no longer be ignored: on runways in Europe and America, models are parading around with an assortment of odd haircuts: seventies shags, frothy mullets, or plain unkempt mops. Creative industries – entertainment, hospitality, advertising, media – are incubating a new breed of hipsters with sideburns and tendrils curling around their necks, as if to prove that they don't live in suburbs or work for banks (even if they do).

The new looks are not really *négligé*, though: they are the product of careful and expensive sculpting, with layers of uneven length. The object is to appear unconcerned but not be so. This is another signifier in the construction of the rather feminine model type – the skinny, pale sensitive guy in a V-neck sweater – who has been the paragon of forward designers for the past two or three years. And note that the new long is not really long, but medium-long: it is just a bit of fringe over your ears, shoulder-length at the most. Hippy-style manes have not yet returned, nor have ponytails.

I am conflicted about this development. It is one of those trends which unfairly discriminates against all but the very young. If your hair is thinning even slightly, if your hairline is receding even minutely, you will look silly sporting a shaggy fringe. So go for it if you have a lot of hair, and can afford the advice of a chic stylist; just keep it clean.

I still recommend the classic short back and sides – à la Cary Grant – for conservative men, and short and spiky (perhaps cut slightly unevenly, or "textured") for the rebellious. A variation of the short back and sides is the **mushroom** or **undercut**, which has one long layer hanging over very short (Number One or Two clipper) sides and back. The mushroom works best with straight hair and gives a rather schoolboyish look. Another perennially popular look, particularly for those with slightly curly hair, is the **caesar**: short, combed forward over the forehead, with small sideburns.

None of these is currently in the most forward loop of fashion, but they will not make you look silly.

And any cut that is long enough to actually move when you shake your head, I leave to the Advanced Class.

Colour

We associate very obviously coloured hair – punky streaks, skaters' dark-roots-and-bleach jobs, gothic boot-polish looks – with street fashion, and therefore with acceptably macho roles such as bicycle courier or snowboarder. There is nothing unmanly about wildly dyed hair – as long as it's obviously fake.

The mullet

We all know the style: the short-in-front, long-in-the-back coiffure beloved of craft-fair organizers and the owners of bait-and-tackle stores. But nobody really knows where this delightful word comes from. I love the word, for even in its etymological vagueness it is such a precise descriptor, with its echoes of both *dullard* and *bullet*, its fish-like flatness. No word could be dumber than *mullet*. The style itself is now returning to fashion as something vaguely ironic and impenetrably in-the-know. Copy it, by all means, if you want to be seen as a vaguely ironic and impenetrably in-the-know person. ❧

Paradoxically, it's the dye job that aims at looking *natural* that tends to make men squirm. We can joke about where we get our tips bleached yellow, but we probably won't joke about our normal-looking dark brown hair if we are hiding the dark secret that its true colour is grey. It's the kind of thing we will whisper about others ("Do you think he *dyes his hair*?") rather than boast about ourselves.

And yet men are hesitating less and less about getting natural-looking dye jobs, just as women always have. Why not? If the technology is available to make you look ten years younger, then you should have no fear in indulging in it. There are now even do-it-yourself kits sold in drugstores targeted specifically at men, such as L'Oreal's Feria line or Redken's Colour Camo for Men, which offer natural blond, auburn, and tawny tones. Someone must be buying them, and it's not just teenage punks.

> "Men are HESITATING less and LESS about getting NATURAL-LOOKING dye jobs."

I would be careful about these kits. First, because false colour always does look a little false. Science still has not perfected the duplication of natural hair pigmentation. And so the more subtle you try to be about this, the more at risk of exposure you are: people will realize that your hair colour is false but you are trying to hide it. And yes, there is a double standard at work here: society at large still has no problem with cosmetics and concealment among women, but does not want to extend this privilege to men. Men who wear makeup or who appear to groom and preen too much are going to be judged, fairly or not, as insubstantial and silly. This is irrational, but there are ways of understanding it: you can understand, for example, that women don't want to go out with men who are prettier than they are. So, if you want to jazz up your hair colours, better to go all out with something wacky or obvious, and you will appear insouciant rather than vain.

Second, there is an inevitable ignominy involved in the bathroom-sink dye job: plastic gloves are involved, and plastic shower caps, and tubes of toxic chemicals. It's messy and it's embarrassing. Most men will be afraid of the process more than they are afraid of the results.

Even if you go to a salon to have it done, you must face that agonizing half-hour under the big roaring 1950s helmet of a hair dryer, with an apron around your neck, while sexy women in tight dresses click past without looking at you. If you are as tense as I am, you will begin to fear that some football-playing hero of your childhood, some bully of long-forgotten playgrounds, will stride in at that very moment, recognize you, and guffaw. If you can face this process with equanimity, then your self esteem is so high and your sexuality so confident that you should run for public office.

Facial Hair

Almost all men in the Western world wore at least a moustache until around the time of the First World War. The war and the Jazz Age destroyed the nineteenth-century traditions, and natty young men in European capitals were resolutely clean-shaven right up until the hippy sixties. There were issues of social class around this as well, and still are, even in these tolerant times. Through much of the twentieth century, any kind of facial hair was anathema to the privileged classes. A moustache alone may have been an entirely respectable military appurtenance, but artistically shaved beards or sideburns have meant jazz musicians, Latinos, or other subversives.

I myself have always snubbed facial growth of any kind, terrified of any kind of visual reference to the sixties, the seventies, the police force, or my lower-middle-class colonial ancestry.

For the proletarian link is definitely there. In Europe and in America, from the upper-middle class upward, facial hair is taboo in practice, never admitted. Kingsley Amis, who was obsessed with class, wrote his last novel about it: in *The Biographer's Moustache*, an aristocratic old curmudgeon scorns his would-be biographer merely because he has a moustache, a sign of working-class origins.

Kingsley Amis was too conservative to be aware of the more modern connotation of the moustache, which is homosexuality. The ultimate military combination – crewcut and moustache – used to be so common a gay look that its adherents were known in the gay world as "clones."

For some reason, a moustache with beard or

"In Europe and in America, from the UPPER-MIDDLE CLASS upward, facial hair is TABOO."

goatee attached does not carry any of these connotations: indeed since the early 1990s, the **Vandyke** –
the moustache attached to a narrow strip of beard
at the chin – has become the badge of the macho
man, of the bouncer and the professional wrestler.
(Funny how fine these lines are.)

It is interesting how rapidly these cycles spin: in
the 1980s, the clean face was the only hip possibility, owing to the persistent influence of British punk
and "New Romantic" musical styles, both of which
were strictly clean-shaven aesthetics, in reaction to
the hirsute, all-natural seventies. Then the seventies
nostalgia began, at the same time as grunge rock,
and all hair broke loose.

The Vandyke – so-called after the popular seven-
teenth-century style often painted by Flemish
master Van Dyck – is often called a **goatee**, although
strictly the goatee is merely the goatlike chin tuft
that forms the bottom half of the Vandyke.

If you have nothing but a little tuft in the hollow
under the lower lip, in the manner of jazz pianist
Thelonious Monk or any number of bicycle couriers, it would be called a **"soul patch."**

All of these more elaborate designs – the Vandyke,
the soul patch, the goatee, the pointy L-shaped sideburns known to some as the "Captain Kirk" – were,
in the 1990s, restricted to inner cities and youthful
musical undergrounds, but have now gained credi-
bility in the suburban world of the beer commercial
and the newscaster. Indeed, I would say that the

combination of Vandyke and crewcut or shaved head is an indicator of the deepest social conservatism.

For this reason, I predict another rapid return, in this decade, to complete shaving among the fashionable. As with most things hair-related, the basic rules apply: if you are ever in doubt, shave it off.

Be aware that moustaches on their own advertise that you are (a) gay or (b) ancient. Which is fine, either way, as long as you are advertising in full consciousness.

Be aware that **full beards** still signal shyness and diffidence. You, on the other hand, want to communicate confidence: go for a close trim. Beards can look clean and stylish as long as you keep them neatly clipped: make sure your neck and your cheekbones are shaved, and that the hair is kept very short. Nobody wants to worry about how much soup is congealed in there.

Shaving

The key to comfortable shaving is heat. A clean cloth soaked in hot water applied to the face for a good minute before you begin, and the use of a hot shaving brush to apply soap, solve half the regularly reported problems: the heat softens the bristles and brings them up for snipping.

An electric razor won't leave you feeling clean and soft and shiny the way a wet shave does

After you have heated and wet your face, apply some soap. People get very serious and scientific about what kind of soap to use: in truth, the discussion is useless because every man's skin is different.

Some faces will go red and blotchy at the touch of all but the most expensive hypoallergenic shaving gels; some are perfectly comfortable with the slathering of a regular bath bar. You have to experiment. Basically, all soaps, gels, and foams have the same function: to provide lubrication for the razor. It's a very simple function, and most soaps perform it in exactly the same way, so don't waste your time worrying about the purported merits of creams with pseudo-scientific properties and chic packaging. I find Ivory Soap works just fine. I slather it on, after the hot water, then soak a shaving brush in more hot water and lather it up on my face.

Shaving brushes can also be an area of great indulgence, but this is an area in which indulgence pays off. There is a difference between cheap bristles and expensive ones: good ones are made with boar's hair, the best are made of pure badger hair, and the very best are of the most soft and delicate badger hair, taken from the animal's chin and underbelly. These can cost several hundred dollars. The finer the brush, the less irritation on your skin.

You shave, of course, with the grain, that is in the direction that the bristles are growing. You may find, however, that on your neck this technique will cause irritation and shaving bumps – those eruptions that signal the beginning of an ingrown or inflamed hair follicle. To avoid this, experiment with shaving against the grain in the problem areas – particularly under your chin and jaw. You would be amazed by how well this counterintuitive procedure solves the problem of the perpetually reddened neck.

After you have finished and rinsed off the excess soap (paying careful attention to your ears, where embarrassing deposits of foam are wont to last all day), you will rinse your face with cold water to close the pores again. You will then apply some kind of moisturizer. The practice of applying an alcohol-based aftershave, said to close the pores, is now frowned on, as the alcohol is astringent: it dries the skin and causes irritation. If it stings, it's probably doing you no good. The purpose of the moisturizer is to keep the skin supple and glowing and young. Again, prices for these things vary widely, but the quality doesn't: they are all variations on grease of some kind. I find that women's moisturizing creams work just as well as men's.

If you find this process too elaborate and finicky, you are probably an electric razor kind of guy. I loathe electric razors myself, as they do not shave nearly as closely, and they don't leave you feeling clean and soft and shiny the way the wet shave does. It's just not a refreshing experience. But if it's the only thing that will enable you to get through the trauma of shaving daily, it's better than nothing.

If you shave, you have to shave *every day*. If you tell yourself that women like the rough two-days-of-stubble look so as to avoid the dull task, you are fooling yourself: your girlfriend may like you looking stubbly and ragged in the confines of your bedroom,

"If you SHAVE, you have to shave *EVERY DAY.*"

or at the cabin, but she will be embarrassed to see you in a restaurant or an office looking like that: she knows it looks puerile and simply negligent. Women want their men to look grown-up, and grown-up men present themselves to the world in a way that shows that they have something important to do. They also show respect for those around them by looking clean. Believe me: the stubbly look is immature. Get over it.

The Body

Why body hair suddenly became undesirable in the mass-media portrayals of masculinity in the late twentieth century is a subject of some fascination for sociologists. All kinds of bogeymen have been blamed: bodybuilding, gay culture, pornography, the cult of youth, Calvin Klein underwear ads. This discussion is pretty aimless, however, as it is impossible to distinguish between a symptom and a cause here – between a reflection of a zeitgeist and a driver of it. Yes, a hairless body makes you look much younger, but why is it that we want men to look like overdeveloped teenagers? Whatever the reason, the culture has demanded its musclemen be hairless for the next few years. Hairy chests have gone the way of moustaches: they have become kitschy symbols of embarrassing pre-1980 fashions. Hairy backs are even worse – symbols of age and outsiderness.

And this provides a great deal of stress for contemporary men. If you ask a group of young women

– women under thirty – what they think of a man with a hairy back, most of them will squeal with disgust. And then if you ask them what they think of a man who waxes his back, you will hear equally enthusiastic expressions of derision. A man who waxes his body seems like a preening narcissist, the dreaded metrosexual, a figure of fun.

So we are caught between caricatures. What are we to do? Do we put ourselves through the cost and discomfort of waxing, or shave, or merely defiantly resist this aesthetic trend? It is, after all, ridiculous to resist a natural and healthy inclination of our bodies – and isn't it a sign of high levels of testosterone, which should be attractive anyway?

This complaint will no doubt bring some grim satisfaction to feminists who have been complaining for decades that feminine body ideals are unnatural and unfair, forcing women to submit to bodily tortures such as starvation and depilation. Now it's the men's turn to face this dilemma. And, interestingly, the evidence shows that they are buckling to pressure in exactly the way women do. In growing numbers, men are going to spas to have their bodies covered with hot wax, which is then torn off, ripping out hairs by the root as it goes. Hands, feet, ears, and noses are also popular spots for depilation.

And perfectly normal men in their teens and twenties are increasingly likely to shave their genitals, as they have seen in pornography, with no sense of excessive vanity: it's just a style. Inevitably, as this generation grows up, the practice will seem less odd to both genders.

Women in their thirties and over are less likely to be turned on by this practice, and less likely generally to want their men to look like teenage models. So feel free to resist the pressure provided by images of shiny, sculpted celebrities in film and print: your life will not necessarily improve if you regain a pre-adolescent smoothness.

A hairy back is still, however, firmly out of fashion. If you feel self-conscious about yours, my advice for dealing with the double standard of female opinion on this is to go ahead and wax it, but quietly. (It will cost you about fifty dollars in a big-city spa; almost all of them accept male clients, and in fact many have regular men's nights once a week.) Do it and keep it a secret. Women want you to look perfect but they don't want to know that you have expended any effort in doing so; they do not want to hear about your grooming routines, or even think about you thinking about it. So don't tell them.

"A hairy BACK is still FIRMLY out of fashion."

CHAPTER THIRTEEN

WORDS TO LIVE BY

A s a summary, and instead of a conclu-sion, here are some guiding principles which will last through any fashion:

- A jacket will always make you feel more confi-dent than a sweater.
- A beautiful shirt and tie make a bigger first impression than an expensive suit does.
- If you are spending more on your car audio com-ponents than on your clothes, your invitations to fabulous parties are probably limited.
- If in doubt about the formality of a social occasion, dress down. You will feel sillier as the only man in a dinner jacket than as the only man in a suit.
- Casual does not mean ugly. It does not mean clothing for mountain exploration. You do not

need Gore-Tex gaiters and lugged soles and emergency flashlights for getting in and out of taxis.

- Diving watches are for diving. Kayaking sandals are for kayaking. Running shoes are for running. Knapsacks are for hiking. Greek fishermen's caps don't even look good on Greek fishermen.

- Black is still the coolest colour for casual wear, despite what anyone who lives in a gated suburb tells you.

- Minimize the keys in your pocket.

- We want to see your suspenders about as much as we want to see your socks and underwear. In a restaurant, if you take your jacket off and hang it on the back of a chair, you will frighten people into thinking you are about to take off your shoes. Who knows where it will end?

- If you wear a baseball cap in a restaurant, your spouse may legally divorce you and retain all your assets.

- If you are losing your hair, cut it shorter.

- No moustaches. No fanny packs strapped to the belly. No tinted spectacles.

- T-shirts given to you for your participation in some event – a folk festival, a fun run, a training seminar, a television studio audience – make excellent paint rags and car-wax buffers.

- Race-car drivers and soccer players are paid large sums of money to wear corporate logos on their clothes. If you are not being paid, why work for free?

- A sports jacket and tie is less formal than a suit and tie. A suit with no tie is less formal than a sports jacket with a tie.
- A suit and tie require leather shoes with leather soles.
- A white shirt is more formal than a coloured or patterned shirt. It is also more boring. If you wear a navy suit with a white shirt and a red tie, you will be mistaken for a Midwestern congressman.
- Increase the spread in your collar and you will suddenly look a little more dashing.
- Nothing rust-coloured looks good.
- Tennis hats look hip and urban on twenty-year-olds. On anyone over forty, they look exactly like Tilley hats, made for gardening in and around your bed-and-breakfast.
- French cuffs are the poor man's sports car, a stellar luxury for a small price. They make you feel rich and powerful, even when you are not.
- For the daring: try clogs. Try a sarong in summer.
- Make sure your shoelaces are parallel, not criss-cross.
- When in doubt about the tastefulness of a new trend, avoid it. When in doubt about your own taste, buy expensive and conservative – and dressy. It is much easier to go wrong with casual clothes.
- Be prepared, whenever you leave the house, to find yourself somewhere cooler than you expected to be. What if someone pulls up in a silver

Mercedes, plucks you out of the parking lot, thrusts a martini into your hand, and introduces you to a countess? Will you be ready?

Above all: Stop feeling guilty about vanity. A sensual pleasure in surfaces is a sign of artistic sensitivity.

Works Consulted

Barr, Ann, and Peter York. *The Official Sloane Ranger Handbook*. London: Ebury Press, 1982.

Chenoune, Farid. *A History of Men's Fashion*. Translated from the French by Deke Dusinberre. Paris: Flammarion, 1993.

Flusser, Alan. *Dressing the Man: Mastering the Art of Permanent Fashion*. New York: HarperCollins, 2002.

———. *Style and the Man: How and Where to Buy Fine Men's Clothes*. New York: HarperCollins, 1996.

Fussell, Paul. *Class: A Guide Through the American Status System*. New York: Touchstone/Simon & Schuster, 1992.

———. *Uniforms: Why We Are What We Wear*. New York: Houghton Mifflin, 2002.

Laver, James. *Costume and Fashion: A Concise History*. London: Thames & Hudson, 1996.

McDowell, Colin, ed. *The Pimlico Companion to Fashion*. London: Pimlico/Random House, 1998.

O'Hara Callan, Georgina. *The Thames & Hudson Dictionary of Fashion and Fashion Designers*. London: Thames & Hudson, 1998.

Roetzel, Bernhard. *Gentleman: A Timeless Fashion*. Translated from the German by Christine Bainbridge, Anthea Bell, Terry Moran, and Martin Pearce. Cologne: Könemann, 1999.

Acknowledgements

Much of this book was first published in a weekly column in the *Globe and Mail*. The column was really the idea and creation of my editor, Dick Snyder, to whom I now owe more than a couple of drinks. I am grateful. Thanks also to the other editors who have helped me with this task: Jill Borra, Cathrin Bradbury, Deborah Fulsang, Jessica Johnson, and Sheree-Lee Olson. And to Alex Schultz, who vastly and sensitively improved this manuscript.

My most important technical adviser is Craig Dellio, who has patiently shared his expertise with me. Mr. Dellio's father, Perry Dellio, founded the store that is now Perry's Yorkville, in Toronto, one of the few remaining small-scale tailoring establishments with knowledge of every sartorial tradition. I am grateful to father and son for their taste and generosity.

In the years of writing the weekly column, I was helped frequently and enthusiastically by other professionals in the clothing industry, who always responded to my requests for information without hesitation, even when their shops were full of paying clients. Many retailers and salesmen shared their time and expertise with me with no demands for recognition. I am grateful to them all, but would like to single out a couple in particular: Nicolas

Kalatzis, of the chic Nicolas store, in Toronto, makes a delicious espresso, and has always had time to serve me one while chatting about hem lengths and button stances. Finally, Harry Rosen and his son Larry Rosen, of the large Harry Rosen chain, have selflessly shared their great knowledge with me in extremely gentlemanly fashion. I like to think that generosity of spirit and aesthetic taste go hand in hand; these guys are my evidence.

Although a great deal of the factual information in this book has been shamelessly lifted from conversations with these men, all errors are my own.

My greatest thanks go to my parents, Ann and Rowland Smith: my mother's impeccable fashion sense has shaped mine, and my father's knowledge is the basis of this book.

Index

The annotation (s) refers to sidebars. References to illustrations are in italic.